01

MW00814812

101 Antiques and Collectibles Trivia Tips That Can Make You Rich, Famous, and the Hit of the Party

Betcha Didn't Know That!

VOL. 1

Leon Castner
And
Brian Kathenes

To Luke, my one of my most favorite people in the world. Enjoy.

★ With Special Bonus Section ★

Betcha Didn't Know That!
101 Antiques and Collectibles Trivia Tips
That Can Make You Rich, Famous, and the Hit of the Party
Volume 1
Leon Castner
and
Brian Kathenes
"With Special Bonus Section"

Published by:
National Appraisal Consultants, LLC
Post Office Box 482
Hope, NJ, 07844
(908) 459-5996
e-mail: TheUglyGuys@BrianAndLeon.com
www.ValueThisRadio.com

ISBN: 978-1-60097-002-3
LCCN: 2007937021

Cover design and layout by NZ Graphics, www.nzgraphics.com

Printed in the United State of America

First Edition

TABLE OF CONTENTS

"I am mainly known for producing antiques and collectibles price guides which appeal to those wonderful sentiments of nostalgia and the need to know how much something is worth. What Leon and Brian have reminded me is that what we also love is the colorful characters and the humor which are so much part of the reason we love this business."

~ Judith Miller, Publisher, The Price Guide Company

Dedication and Acknowledgements

I'D LIKE TO dedicate this effort to my father, Don Castner, who never stopped learning and sharing experiences with all he met. He always did his very best in whatever venture he undertook and showed me that faith and antiques mix as well as anything else.

I would like to thank my wife Monica for her support and encouragement and also my children-all seven of them (Bonnie, Christine, Barbra, Karen, Maria, Jonathan, and Daniel) for helping with the auctions whether they wanted to or not and for always treating my profession with dignity and respect—even though none of them wanted to pursue it.

I also want to thank Brian for being the sounding board and foil to my remarks and jests. His good spirit and high enthusiasm will always make me seem like an Eeyore to a Tigger!

~ Leon

THIS BOOK IS dedicated to Gunnar Kathenes, the most honest man I know. He taught me, at a young age, that I could achieve any goal, no matter how challenging, as long as I was willing to do the work to get there. I also learned from him and his positive example, that doing the right thing all the time makes life a whole lot easier and less complicated. His unselfish dedication to our family, and to others, always inspires me and also inspires everyone who knows him. Thanks Dad!

A special world of thanks goes out to my lovely and wonderful wife Nancy, for her love and guidance. And a big time 'shout out' to Tyler and Lee, for their hard work around the office, and for being the coolest kids on the planet. Thanks guys!

Finally, my sincere appreciation and thanks goes to my business partner and good friend Leon Castner. Leon really got me into this business—(you'll pay for that someday, Leon). His dedication to the profession, along with his incredible knowledge and superb guidance have a huge impact on my success.

~ Brian

Introduction

WELCOME TO THE wonderful, and often wacky, world of antiques and collectibles - also known as the wonderful, and often wacky, world of Brian and Leon, two guys with different and diverse backgrounds (an engineer and a theologian), who joined forces years ago to form an appraisal company that eventually worked on such strange cases as the Nixon Watergate Papers and the bankruptcy of a major east coast college.

Brian's specialty is really autographs, historical documents, rare books, celebrity memorabilia and unusual collectibles. Leon's domain is all the rest (he was also an auctioneer). Together we surround ourselves with experts and work it all out. Our combined experience constitutes over sixty years. Or is it one year of experience repeated sixty times? Whatever the case, it's safe to say, we've seen it all and done most of it. Let us tell you—it's a strange world!

Both of us love the field of antiques and collectibles; This is not to say that we scour the countryside in an attempt to purchase and own one-of-a kind examples of great craftsmanship and beauty to display in our gorgeous townhouses while holding important cocktail parties to impress our friends and clients (if we had any). Rather, we know a lot about this field because we enjoy the process of discovery and are genuinely interested in the history and background of the objects that we uncover in our never ending quest.

Not only do old and unusual items surprise and astound us, but often the circumstances surrounding their creation and use, catch us off guard and provide us glimpses of historical interest, human predicament, and comical delight.

This short compendium of recent radio show tidbits taken from our daily Value This! radio show 'promo' called "Betcha' Didn't Know That" demonstrates the variety and scope of human interest stories surrounding the world of collecting-from penny postcards to the Eiffel Tower (how does one collect Eiffel Towers?)

It is not meant as a systematic history, a scholarly treatise (what, us scholars?!), or an encyclopedia of any sort, nor is it a price guide, an appraiser's handbook, or a coffee table book (it's not big enough).

We do hope it serves as an enjoyable, leisurely hike through a pleasant, yet sometimes confusing territory that demands more attention. Pick this up when you have time, read a few pages, smile, and set it down. (It's hard to take more than a few pages of us at one sitting). When you are bored, dive back into the book. We guarantee another smile, or at least an admission, "Gee, I didn't know that."

It's fodder for the barbershop, chit chat for the water cooler, or trivia for your next party. Hopefully you'll find a few things here that you didn't know, a bunch you did (but forgot), and some that you thought you knew but didn't have a clue as to the real story. For everything has a story...

Betcha Didn't Know That!

~ Brian and Leon

Disclaimer: Information in this book has been gathered from a variety of resources and should not be considered the "last word" on any price, item, or topic.

We all know that the following is true: prices change – markets change – interests change. What's hot today may be trash tomorrow. So before you run out to buy or sell anything based upon what you've read in this book, do a bit more research, or better yet, visit our website to learn more about the value of your stuff: www.BestCollectibleTips.com

While attempts have been made to verify the information provided in this publication, neither the authors nor the publisher assume any responsibility for errors, inaccuracies, or omissions. Any slights of people, groups, or organizations are unintentional.

This publication is not intended for use as a source of legal or accounting information and should not be used as such. Rather, appropriate professionals should be consulted. All information in this publication is subject to all federal, state, and/or local laws and regulations. All users of this information must be certain all appropriate laws and regulations are followed.

The authors and publisher assume no responsibility or liability whatsoever on behalf of any purchaser, reader or user of these materials.

BASEBALL: THE AMERICAN PASTTIME

~ ABOUT BASEBALL ~

"Baseball is 90% mental; the other half is physical."
~ Yogi Berra

SPORTS COLLECTIBLES ARE among the hottest in the field (no pun intended). They're also among the most reproduced, copied, and faked of all items. It has been estimated that 90% of all sports memorabilia is either falsified or simply wrong. Not surprising, baseball takes the biggest hit (no pun intended).

Collecting baseball cards was a big deal in the 1950's. Both Brian and I remember spending a nickel to get a bunch of cards AND the bubble gum (the best part). Cards were quickly examined and discarded. Maybe one out of the whole lot was saved (because it was a Yankee), only to be traded, flipped, or perhaps clipped to a bike frame near the spokes to create instant muffler sounds.

We saved them, but not for monetary purposes. They were part of our childhood, our playthings. Believe it or not-we actually handled them. We drew faces, mustaches, and X's on players after bad games. We even read the backs (yes, they have backs). Our storage area was a shoe-box, and our moms were constantly telling us to clean up our messes and put the cards away.

If nothing else, "baseball cards" created the whole new category in the world of collectibles. No one had heard of a Honus Wagner card (and nobody cared) until they started writing books and indexes (lists of all cards ever made). Once someone assigned a value to a card (a made it a business instead of a hobby), the game changed (pun intended).

Cards became like money. You could still barter (like we always did), but now you could also buy and sell. You didn't even have to like or dislike a player or team! Someone, somewhere, was telling us that the value of a card was worth a whole lot more than we had in our pockets. They were also telling us that saving them would be like putting money in our little metal banks shaped like Yankee Stadium. Someday, we might be RICH!

Most of the baseball cards we collected weren't that old. As a matter of fact, our parents didn't even know or care about them because they weren't their playthings when they were kids. Since age was relatively unimportant, we evaluated our cards based on the condition in which we kept them: messy, average, or tip top shape. The better preserved the cards, the higher the value they maintained. What better excuse did we need to keep things neat?

That 'condition' factor, we later learned, became the fundamental ingredient to any collectible item, particularly any item that was mass-produced and was not 100 years old. So markets changed, the hobby changed, our perceptions changed, and the world of the baseball collectible became "official." Gone were the days of innocence.

Just like baseball players' salaries, the price of cards and other memorabilia has steadily risen. The game has become more than a pastime and a young boy's dream. It has become the American dream—the one about finding a bargain and striking it rich.

Make Games Not War

WAR IS HELL. But can it be fun, too? No, although a Civil War general was able to capture the hearts of Yankee soldiers while they were chasing Johnny Reb.

Abner Doubleday, a general in the Civil War, may not have made a name for himself on the field of battle, but on the baseball field, he became an

American icon (albeit a somewhat modest one.)

When Abner was a cadet at West Point when he mapped out the first baseball diamond.

In 1863, as major general of volunteers, Doubleday fought at Gettysburg and oversaw the playing of his favorite game: baseball.

Surprisingly, despite the fact that Doubleday left behind numerous diaries, he never claimed to have invented baseball.

Ol' Abner is a beloved figure and his papers and writings are pretty well-loved, too. A letter from the general to his brother, discussing the possibility of a Confederate invasion of Washington, D.C., sold for over $10,000.

That's what we'd call a grand slam…make that a ten-grand slam!

> The Mills Commission was appointed in 1905 to discover the true origin of our game called baseball. Their final report credited Abner Doubleday as the inventor of the game in Cooperstown, New York in 1839. However, there no evidence to support the claim. In 1839, Doubleday was a cadet at West Point, and there is no record of him traveling to Cooperstown. Moreover, none of his letters or papers indicate his involvement in the game. So, if Doubleday can get credit for inventing baseball without any recorded history, perhaps we (Leon & Brian) can get credit for inventing the call in antiques radio talk show.

Bobbleheads

WE'RE NOT TALKING about Brian and Leon—we're talking about small figures that move their heads (we are talking about Brian and Leon). They're called bobbing heads, wobblers, or bobbleheads.

Sports bobbleheads first appeared on the baseball scene in the 1950's. They were paper machete figures, about 4 or 5 inches tall, that had stationary bodies and a spring that fastened the head. Any slight movement would cause the head to move back and forth, up or down, or just "bobble."

Among the first were a series produced in 1960. They included Roberto Clemente, Mickey Mantle, Roger Maris, and Willie Mays. The unusual thing was that they all had the same face. Only the uniform colors and numbers were different.

The most famous of the bobbleheads weren't baseball players at all. They were the Beatles. The famous set of four (with different heads) can command hundreds and even thousands of dollars.

The phenomenon ended as quickly as most players and by the mid 70's it was gone.

It wasn't until 1999 that the bobbleheads reappeared. At a San Francisco Giants game honoring Willie Mays, 35,000 units were given away. These were plastic and they did have the correct head. Ever since they've become the giveaway of choice.

The interesting tidbit, which is what we are all about, is the fact that the bobblehead is not really a baseball or sports invention. In fact, it isn't even a 20th century one.

Bobbleheads were originally called nodders, nodding figures, or even pagods. Most were Asian and had porcelain or pottery figures with wires that attached the hands and heads. Any movement, even air, would cause the figure to move-creating a lifelike appearance.

The differences between the old nodders and the newer bobbleheads are easy to spot. Here are some guidelines:

1. The old were usually not made of plastic.
2. The old had wires rather than a spring.
3. The old didn't look like Willie Mays or Paul McCartney.

Now how's that for bobblehead advice? (Just nod your head up and down.)

Yankees vs. Mummies

THE MILLS COMMISSION was a group created to determine the "paternity" of baseball. As previously stated, it concluded that Abner Doubleday did, indeed, invent baseball.

Well, with all due respect to the Commission, Abner may have invented *American* baseball, but the cry of "batter up" was probably first been heard around 4,000 years ago in ancient Mesopotamia.

We weren't there for Opening Day, but we hear that the ancient Egyptians are the earliest people to have fooled around with bats and balls.

Pharaohs played seker-hemat, which is loosely translated as "batting the ball." We surmise they used their priests as catchers. Who else would have the patience to endure getting "nailed" by King Tut's wild pitches day after day?

The game may have been different, but the "heart" was the same. Baseball, then and now, reminds us of "renewal" each spring. We can identify with, and are inspired by the achievements of baseballs' heroic figures. Consequently, baseball has become a conduit for national and even political loyalty.

> **More than Just a Game**
> Batting the ball was part of religious ceremonies in Egypt...and perhaps that's the origin of our "religion" of baseball! On the other hand, maybe the Egyptians invented the "other" baseball game—the one played in England. Since they loved beetles, bugs, and scarabs, and even made jewelry out of them, doesn't it make sense they would have invented a game called...CRICKET!

Did you think baseball was just about strikes and balls? Think again.

It's the stuff that dreams—and *Fields of Dreams*—are made of.

A Bonus For Honus

BASEBALL CARDS. YOU can collect 'em... You can swap 'em... *And* you can sell 'em for BIG bucks—if you know what to look for.

The "mother" of all baseball cards is the Honus Wagner T-206 tobacco card. One was sold recently for $2.5 million!

Tobacco card? That's right tobacco!

The first baseball cards didn't come with chewing gum for the kiddies, folks. They were used to promote tobacco products to the big boys.

In the late 1800's, "trade cards" were used by merchants and salesmen to advertise their wares and their store addresses. The cards were attractive and eye-catching...not to mention free...so they immediately became collectibles.

And speaking of phenomenon, let's get back to our man behind the plate...

John Peter "Honus" Wagner—known as "The Flying Dutchman"—is considered one of the greatest shortstops in history. He was one of the first five players to be inducted into the Baseball Hall of Fame.

Peck and Snyder

You've heard of Sears and Roebuck, Abraham and Strauss, Brian and Leon...but do you know Peck and Snyder? P&S manufactured baseball equipment after the Civil War and advertised their products with **trade cards** featuring prominent baseball players of the day. P&S's cards were different from today's **trading cards** that carry no advertising, just pix and stats.

Honus is a baseball great, but it's not his maneuvering between the bags that make the Wagner T206 tobacco card the *Mona Lisa* of baseball cards. It's their rarity.

Why so rare??

It seems Honus objected to the use of his name to promote smoking, without being properly compensated. He demanded that the manufacturer—the American Tobacco Company—stop production.

They're as rare as a triple play! Only 50 or 60 Honus Wagner cards were ever distributed.

Triple Play

WHICH PLAYER IN baseball history could be in three different Hall of Fames? Give up?

We'll tell you. It's Ted Williams.

Ted Williams, undoubtedly one of the best baseball players ever to play the game, is best known for his status as a member of the **Boston Red Sox.** He won the American League batting crown when he was 39 and 40 and he was the last 400 hitter in 1941. (That means a guy gets a hit almost every other time he faces a pitcher.) He won the Triple Crown twice (most hits, home runs, and best average). That's pretty good.

His entrance to Cooperstown was a no-brainer.

Many of us "know" Ted, particularly baby boomers, not as a ballplayer, since he ended his playing in 1960, but as another sportsman—a fisherman! Yep, believe it or not, Ted became a mad "basser". He spent his later years trawling for fish in the swamps, rivers, and oceans of the world and was among the first to televise his feats. (Who said fishing wasn't a sport?) He was inducted into the Fishing Hall of Fame.

The third sport is really not a sport at all. (You knew it all along.)

When WWII broke out in the 1940's, many players left the ball fields and served on other fields. Ted's was an airfield. He served as a marine pilot and won an honor or two as he served his country in another way. When he came back, he started where he left off, challenging pitchers and whacking the ball. A few short years later, another conflict broke out, this time in Korea, and, sure enough, Ted met the call. We're not sure, but he might be one of the only players to have served in both wars and came home to continue playing.

Although we don't think there's a Pilot Hall of Fame (except for up in the ski with Snoopy and the Red Baron), if there is, Ted's probably in it.

So here's to Ted, wherever he might be (in Arizona or in the big game in the sky). A triple crown...a triple play. Either way, a miraculous achievement.

> P.S. Note that Ted signed his autographs with his playing name "Ted Williams." He used his more formal signature, Theodore, for legal documents. That's why the debate over his final remains is unclear. The signature on the letter authorizing cryonics instead of cremation was signed "Ted Williams."

The M&M Boys

THE RECENT BIG league battle among the heavyweight home run hitters Mark McQuire and Sammy Sosa had nothing over the original contest in the summer of 1961 between the two "Ms"—Roger Maris and Mickey Mantle.

Maris, a Midwestern kid from Fargo, North Dakota, broke into the big leagues in 1958. After a short stint as a rookie he soon found himself with the mighty New York Yankees. In no time flat he proceeded to hit the long ball. His first full season in New York in 1960 he ended up with just one less four-bagger than Mantel-the hometown favorite.

The following year became the attack of the Ms. It was #7 and #9. One after the other—not in the same league but in the same uniform!

The media—as we all know—loves a contest, particularly when you can pit two opposing teams, styles, or even personalities. Maris, the clean cut (he sported a "butch" or crew cut) upstart versus Mickey, the free-living darling of the team. Even though there was no real animosity between the two (just ask Yogi), the media portrayed Maris as sullen and uncommunicative. Mantle, the pride of Oklahoma, was not much better but became pictured as the "bright" idolized star. Since he had been with the Yankees longer his status both in the clubhouse and stands was much higher.

The beginning of the year started out as a dog race. One from the left (usually Maris) and one from the right (Mantle). Then two from the left (Maris and Mantle). Back and forth until it became clear that one of them might hit the record. Suddenly Mantle went down with a leg injury and there went the fun. (It wasn't until the end of the season that Mickey got back on track and gave Maris some late inning competition.)

Now we were left with a relatively unknown and silent power slugger going against the most famous Yankee of all time-the Babe. As fall neared, it became apparent that it might actually happen. Now the fans were angry. It was one thing to pit two rising stars against each other but quite another to have one defy the bambino. The media and fans reacted with hostility. Maris was no Mantle and he certainly was no Ruth.

His 61st was hit against the Red Sox (had to get that in) in a 1-0 game that led the Yankees to the series and another championship. Maris, new world record holder, had won the battle but lost the war.

In a few short years the heroics had been bitterly forgotten, or at least buried. Maris had been traded to St. Louis to end his career and Mickey…well, he was still Mickey. The M&M boys had ceased to exist—except in the minds of all the fans of that fantastic year.

Not much exists in the collectible field that depicts that colossal battle, but I remember treasuring my Hartland plastic Mickey Mantel figure with a big yellow bat. I never seemed to want the one with the big number 9. So, just for heck of it I looked on eBay. The Maris figure was up to $450. I found a Mantle one for $300. Who knows?

The First Presidential "Pitch"

THIS BASEBALL SEASON, like most baseball seasons of the past, started with the President of the United States tossing out the first pitch of the season to commemorate "Opening Day." It's an American tradition. But where and when did that tradition start?

Perhaps it started with the first President, George Washington.

NOT! Duh – You just read that the game wasn't invented until 1839. Aren't you paying attention??

OK then. maybe it was Martin Van Buren who threw out the first pitch. He was the President in 1839.

Nope, not him either.

Actually it was President Warren G. Harding who tossed out the first historic pitch on April 13, 1921.

The story goes that President Harding was having a particularly tough day in 'the Oval Office' and needed to get out for a bit. What better place to go to forget your worries than to a baseball game. He dropped in on the Washington Senators game and was asked to toss out the first ball of the season. Harding started a tradition that that continues to this day.

Incidentally, the Senators were playing the Red Sox that day and were soundly defeated 6 to 3.

Babe Ruth was not at that game. He had been traded by the Red Sox to the Yankees two years earlier. Nevertheless, he did make an appearance against the Senators at Yankee Stadium on April 4, 1923. Harding attended that game too. Unfortunately, that didn't help the Senators. The Yankees shutout the Senators 4 – zip. The Babe hit a home run and the Yankees earned their first shutout in Yankee Stadium history.

Popular or Traditional Things to Collect

ABOUT ANTIQUES, COLLECTIBLES, AND MEMORABILIA

~ Something For Everyone! ~

"WHAT SHOULD I collect?" is perhaps the most common question asked by callers to our weekly radio show, *Value This!! with Brian and Leon.* Our answer is simple: *"Collect what you like and you'll never go wrong!"*

Some people collect to gain knowledge. Others want to recapture their childhood or remember a simpler time. Still others are looking to make a killing in the business and believe that those rare and strange stories of the million dollar painting purchased at a local flea market for a dollar will happen to them.

The truth is, most of us will never discover a million dollar painting or even a super antique bargain. But, if you collect what you like, you will be more interested in learning more about that subject. By reading, listening, asking questions and researching, you will become an expert in the field of a specific item. And the one who knows more always has an edge in any market. So naturally, you will be able to spot those rare bargains with when they present themselves.

AUTOGRAPHS, COLLECTIBLES & MEMORABILIA: THE ECLECTIC LIFE

Autographs: Will The Mystery Guest Please Sign In?

About Autographs

THE HOBBY OF autograph collecting grew explosively in the 1980s. Autograph shops, historical document galleries, and website autograph stores popped up like mushrooms on a muggy day. Auction houses in big cities and tiny villages are offered autographs of Presidents, movie stars, sports figures, scientists, astronauts and authors. Today autograph collectors can be found in every state in the US and around the world.

Autograph collecting is not new however. Cicero was a collector. Queen Victoria had an extensive collection including signatures of many early Presidents and world leaders. Likewise, Franklin Roosevelt and John F. Kennedy were autograph collectors too.

With all this popularity and interest in autographs, the new collector and even the experienced dealer must take great care in selecting and purchasing autographed material. Both collector and dealer each face an increasingly difficult job of identification and valuation. Multiple markets, title questions, and authenticity concerns all contribute to the confusion and challenges of collecting autographs and historical documents.

Literally millions of dollars worth of rare paper are cast aside and over-looked by collectors, appraisers, insurance adjusters, and their owners every year. Thousands of valuable letters, historical documents, and autographed books are considered by untrained appraisers and dealers as "worthless junk."

Recently, a client asked an antique dealer if his box of old paper had any value. The antique dealer told him the contents were "garbage." Just on a hunch, the client discussed the collection with a qualified appraiser of rare paper autographs and manuscripts. With proper research and investigation, the appraiser determined that the collection contained historically important letters, books, and photographs. One letter alone was valued at over $5,000.00. The collection sold for well over $20,000.00—not bad for a box of junk. The interesting aspect of the collection is that the most valuable letter in it was only 40 years old.

Most people believe that the paper must be very old to have any kind of value, but this is obviously not true. The Jackie Kennedy sale and the Marilyn Monroe auction are two examples of contemporary material being sold for astronomical prices.

It is also important to note that there are a great number of forgeries and facsimile signatures in existence as well. There are far more facsimile signatures and forgeries around than there are genuine examples.

With millions of dollars worth of autographs, manuscripts, books, and photographs around, chances are pretty good that there may be something sitting in your attic, or home; or there may be a document on a table at a garage sale near you. Some of it's good and some of it's not. Make sure you know the difference and are familiar with value before you spend a penny.

There are a number of "identification rules" in autograph collecting. The number one rule: "Assume it is not real until proven otherwise." We all want to believe that we have made a great find. It is in our nature to want to discover a treasure for a fraction of the actual price. Still, not only do you need a keen eye, but you also need a clear head to make this kind of lucrative purchase.

So read on and learn more about autographs, manuscripts, and historical documents, then start searching for the hidden treasures in your neighborhood.

The Man Who Drew Too Much

ALTHOUGH WRITER CLEMENTE Moore described a jelly-bellied Santa in his poem *Twas the Night Before Christmas*, it was artist Thomas Nast who truly brought the beloved character to life.

Nast, born in Germany, was unable to read English. His wife read Moore's poem to the artist to inspire him.

As a staff artist on "Harper's Weekly" from 1862-1866, he used that inspiration to give America some of its most recognized images: the Republican elephant, the Democratic donkey…and the American version of Santa Claus.

Nast's drawings defined Santa as fat, jolly, bearded, and red-suited. But he did more than change the "shape" of Santa. He changed the shape of Christmases to come.

He was the first to "house" Santa at the North Pole and the first to give him a workshop with busy little elves.

The custom of sending Santa a letter can also be traced to Nast, but that's another story. And although the custom of kissing under mistletoe was known in Europe, it was through Nast's engravings in America that the custom caught on here.

(It's one of Brian's favorites!)

And here's a biggie: prior to Nast's engravings, all children received gifts from Santa. Nast conceived the idea that bad children would not receive gifts from Santa.

Nast's writings are just as valuable as his drawings. A short handwritten letter from Nast was recently sold for $2,999.00.

That must have been a Merry Christmas for someone!

Take Me To Your Holograph

ASK LEON "WHAT'S a holograph?" and he'll say, "It's all Greek to me."

He's right!

Holograph come from the Greek words "graph" (writing) and "holo" (with the hand).

Ask Daniel Webster, and the old dictionary writer would probably reply, "It's a document written entirely in the handwriting of the person whose signature it bears." Way to go, Dan!

And although you might be tempted to confuse them with holoGRAMS, holoGRAPHS are a very collectible kind of autograph.

While he was in office, President Lyndon Johnson may have signed lots of legislation, but he hardly ever wrote anything entirely by hand. That's why an LBJ holograph letter may be worth 10 times more than a similar piece of correspondence produced on a typewriter, but with his signature.

(Remember, in Lyndon's day, they didn't use computers the same way we do!!)

Autograph factoids that will help you identify real signatures from the fakes

THE FIRST PRESIDENT to use a ball point pen was John F. Kennedy, so if you find a Herbert Hoover signature written in ball point pen, you can be certain it's a forgery.

Abraham Lincoln hated the name "Abe." He signed his name; "A. Lincoln" or "Abraham Lincoln." So if someone offers you a love letter signed "Your lover boy Abe," you can be pretty sure it not signed by the sixteenth president of the United States.

That Face, That Face, That Fabulous Face

YOU HEAR A lot about artists and their "muses," but we know one Frenchman who didn't have to go any further than his own backyard to find the inspiration for one of the greatest monuments in America.

No…not Mount Rushmore! (Although those are some fabulous faces). We're talking about the Statue of Liberty.

Before coming "home" to America, the colossal head of Lady Liberty was on display at the Paris Exposition of 1878. Naturally! After all, she was created by a Frenchman and inspired by French women.

Frederic Auguste Bartholdi, the French sculptor who created the Lady of the Harbor, modeled his creation on the two favorite women in his life—his wife and his mother!

Mrs. Bartholdi was "the body"—she probably posed wrapped in a bed sheet, holding her hairbrush high in the air. But it was Mama Bartholdi—Charlotte—who put a face on Liberty.

Talk about having a "big head!" Lady Liberty's cranium space can accommodate up to 40 visitors at a time!

And if he were still alive, Bartholdi would probably have a "big head," too…thanks to the value placed on the famous sculptor's autograph.

His signature on a letter discussing his mother and the Statue of Liberty is sold for more than $3,000.

Let freedom…and cash registers…ring!

Gustav's Grand Tour

WHEN MOST LADIES need a little support, they head for the "unmentionables" department to find something in their size.

But in 1886, there was a lady who was so well-endowed that a call went out across France for a man to "engineer" a solution.

The lady? Why the Statue of Liberty, of course!

Created by Frederic Bartholdi and composed of over 8 million pounds of copper panels, the Statue of Liberty was too flimsy to stand on its own. (Ooops!) Bartholdi was forced to call upon an engineer to create some kind of internal support.

The "miracle man" who saved the day did so a little grudgingly as he had other things on his mind…a "tour" (that's French for "tower") to commemorate the centennial of French Independence.

But he created an iron skeleton for the statue and reassembled the sculpture in the United States. Then it was back to Paris to complete his grand

> Gustav's work as an engineer did not end with the Eiffel Tower and the Statue of Liberty.
> He designed and built many structures. He was certainly ahead of his time. He was the first person to propose digging a tunnel under the English Channel and creating an underground Paris rail system.
> Nobody took him up on the offer, so we figure he decided to scrap the idea and just eat lots of French Fries and French Toast.

"tour" and the Paris landmark that still bears his name...

Come on. You know what we're talking about. Say it with us. It's Gustav Eiffel's tower. Or just Eiffel Tower to its friends!

The Long and the Short of William Henry Harrison

IT WAS A dark and stormy night...

No, actually, it was a dark and stormy day when 68-year-old William Henry Harrison, the 9th President of the United States, took his oath of office on the steps of the Capitol building...

Harrison delivered his inauguration address under rainy skies, but he refused to wear a hat or overcoat. (William, what did your mother tell you?!)

He stood outside for the entire proceeding, dressed only in his suit coat. When the speech was over, Harrison greeted crowds of well-wishers at the White House and attended several celebrations that evening.

Apparently, it was too much for "Old Tippecanoe." He contracted pneumonia, and by April, he was dead.

So President Harrison has two "stars" beside his name in the record book: the longest inaugural speech ever presented—one hour and 45 minutes—and the shortest term in office—just 32 days.

> Harrison stated: "Called from a retirement which I had supposed was to continue for the residue of my life to fill the chief executive office of this great and free nation, I appear before you, fellow-citizens, to take the oaths which the Constitution prescribes..."
>
> "Hey, it's freezing out here! I should have worn my hat—I feel a cold coming on."
>
> (OK, we added the last line about the cold just to see if you were paying attention).

Longest...shortest...and most valuable. Since WHH's term in office was so short, he didn't have the opportunity to sign many Presidential papers. That's why his Presidential signature is so scarce and worth so much...

Recently, a Presidential pardon signed by Harrison while in office sold for $110,000!

Hot Button

THERE WERE FIFTY-six soon-to-be-Americans who signed off on the Declaration of Independence.

Don't worry; this isn't history class. We won't ask you to name them all...

But we *will* ask you to guess the name of the signer whose NON-Declaration signature brings in more than $100,000.00 at auction!

It's not who you think...not John Hancock, Tom Jefferson or one of the Adams boys (John or Sam). It's not even Ben Franklin.

Nope, it's the hot-tempered Button Gwinnett, one of three Georgia delegates to the Continental Congress, whose autograph is in huge demand.

To collectors, an original ink-quilled Gwinnett signature would be valued only behind the likes of Julius Caesar and William Shakespeare, making his, by far, the most valuable American autograph in existence.

At last count, there were only 51 known examples of this early American's autograph. The fiery Gwinnett died in a pistol duel less than a year after signing the Declaration. Then, most of his papers were burned in a house fire, so very few of his signatures exist.

A two-line document written in Gwinnett's hand and signed by the Georgian was sold for $135,000 in 1990.

We know quite a few freelance writers and editors who'd like to be paid by the word this way!

Government Grant

YOU CAN'T FOOL us. We know that the answer to the question "Who's buried in Grant's Tomb?"

It's Ulysses S. Grant, the 18th President of the United States.

But the answer to the question "Who signed Grant's memoirs?" is a little trickier.

After he left office, Grant fell on hard times and lost his fortune to corrupt politicians and sleazy businessmen. Faced with cancer and watching his finances dwindle, he decided to write and publish the story of his life and military career so that his family wouldn't be left completely penniless.

Grant's memoirs became immediate bestsellers and have never been out of print since they were first published in the fall of 1886. The publisher was Mark Twain, who described Grant's work as, "The best [memoirs] of any general's since Caesar."

The two-volume set bears the inscription "These volumes are dedicated to the American soldier and sailor" followed by the signature "U.S. Grant." A common set, in great condition, is valued at about $350.

$350.00 For a Presidential signature? What's up with that?

Here's the "inside story"...

The President's signature appears on the front flyleaf of each published edition. But although Grant finished the manuscript before his death, Twain didn't publish it until after the President was gone.

Warning!! There are a number of very common facsimile Presidential Signatures. Presidents "wrote" to many of their constituents using pre-printed letters and signatures. Some of the most common examples include:
- Herbert Hoover's Thank you note for 'kind birthday greeting.'
- Harry Truman's post-presidential letter.
- Presidential Christmas cards.
- And, watch out for all those facsimile copies of Abraham Lincoln's Gettysburg Address. They are still being repro-duced on fake parchment for museum gift shops all over the world.

The signature in every volume is not really a signature at all. It's a "facsimile signature" that was printed right along with the book.

Documents actually signed by Grant are valuable. A rare telegram from Grant to General William T. Sherman, about preparations for the march to the sea, sold for $14,000. (Now that's more like it!)

HAIL TO THE CHIEF

~ ABOUT AMERICAN PRESIDENTS ~

"The President is merely the most important among a large number of public servants. He should be supported or opposed exactly to the degree which is warranted by his good conduct or bad conduct, his efficiency or inefficiency in rendering loyal, able, and disinterested service to the Nation as a whole. Therefore it is absolutely necessary that there should be full liberty to tell the truth about his acts, and this means that it is exactly necessary to blame him when he does wrong as to praise him when he does right. Any other attitude in an American citizen is both base and servile..."

~ Teddy Roosevelt

THE PRESIDENTS OF the United States of America are the most recognized figures in American history.

Each President represents a specific time in our history and captures a snapshot of our culture and the state of our society.

They are associated with many 'firsts.' Andrews Jackson was the first president to ride on a train. William McKinley was the first President to ride in an automobile.

Theodore Roosevelt was the first president to fly in an airplane, but he did it after he left office. He was also the first President to go underwater in a submarine, in Oyster Bay, Long Island near his Sagamore Hill home.

Each Commander in Chief has led our military in peace and in war. George Washington is known as the Indispensable Man. Abraham Lincoln is credited with saving the Union.

Kennedy is associated with the Cuban Missile Crisis, Nixon with Vietnam, FDR with the beginning of World War II and Truman with its atomic end.

Presidential memorabilia encompasses such an amazing variety of time frames, historical events, and political climates its no wonder so many people collect it.

White House dinnerware, Presidential Christmas cards, manuscripts, fabric from White House drapes, campaign ephemera, mass cards, and hats are some of the many Presidential items one can collect.

Some collectors accumulate Ronald Reagan jellybean jars which were flown on Marine One, the Presidential helicopter. Others collect actual pieces of the White House. There is wall covering from the Red Room, granite from the façade and even Presidential hair that can be collected.

There are forty two different President to pick from. Some collectors focus on a particular president, while others want something from each administration.

What ever you collect, you can be sure that in someway it is associated with a particular president or related in some way to his administration.

Death of a President

QUESTION: WHAT'S BLACK and white and 'red' all over?

A sunburned zebra? An embarrassed penguin?

Okay, it was a trick question. It should really read, "What's black and white and READ all over?" And the answer is…

A newspaper.

Now most people think that "yesterday's news" isn't good for much more than wrapping fish. But in truth, the age of the newspaper has very little to do directly with its value.

And if you've got a newspaper with a "hot" story, you'd be better off wrapping those fish in hundred-dollar bills! Depending on the event and the edition you have, you may be throwing away a fortune!

And you don't get much more important than the death of an American President.

The *New York Herald* with the headlines of Lincoln's assassination on April 15, 1865, is another "keeper." It comes in more than twenty reprint variations. Many were produced in the late 1800's and early 1900's.

These reproductions were created as eye-catching advertising flyers and through time became confused with "the real thing." Some are more valuable than others.

But nothing beats a gen-u-wine original.

The *Ulster County Gazette* dated January 4, 1800 contains the obituary of George Washington. An original copy is worth more than $10,000!

Now that's what we call "good news!" (Sorry, George.)

A Picture Is Worth A Thousand Words...and $100,000

NO ONE WOULD call Abe Lincoln "pretty as a picture," but that didn't stop photographers of the time from taking plenty of "snapshots" of the great American president.

Actually, the phrase "snapshots" isn't quite accurate. Honest Abe's face was preserved for all time thanks to the daguerreotype...the world's first successful photographic process.

Daguerreotypes were all the rage in the 1830's. The edition of *The Knickerbocker* newspaper reported, *"Their exquisite perfection almost transcends the bounds of sober belief."*

No wonder everyone from world leaders and successful businessmen to simple soldiers and their families sat for formal portraits!

People who wanted to be captured in a daguerreotype needed the patience of a saint. A subject had to sit motionless for *up to 20 minutes* or the image would be blurred.

Now, with everyone and his brother posing for pictures, you'd think that there would be a rich supply of daguerreotypes from the Civil War era.

No such luck.

Daguerreotypes have disappeared primarily because the surfaces were extremely delicate and easily cracked. And unfortunately, daguerreotypes were one-hit wonders.

They could not be "copied" like today's photo film, so each image is completely unique.

Lincoln daguerreotypes can sell for over $100,000. So it stands to reason that if a Lincoln daguerreotype is worth a cool hundred-grand, then daguerreotypes of the first American president would be worth even more…right?

Wrong!

The father of our country was six-feet-under in 1799…almost thirty years before the daguerreotype was invented.

(It was a trick question.)

In the Kingdom of Auctions, The Last Shall Be The First

ISN'T IT NICE to know that you can be last, but still be a winner?

Okay, this doesn't really apply to the race for the gold at the Olympics, but as far as manuscripts are concerned…especially an Abraham Lincoln manuscript…being last makes you first when it comes to value.

Lincoln's first known writing sample—an 1824 arithmetic book that Abe penned when he was just a fifteen-year-old "pup"—sold for $130,000 in 1991. (The irregularly shaped page contained three different samples of the future Commander-in-Chief's signature.)

Compare that to the value of a "regular" handwritten Lincoln letter: about $10,000.

But it's Lincoln's last public address that's proven to be first in the hearts of collectors, including Malcolm Forbes.

Business mogul Malcolm Forbes was as passionate about words and ideas as he was about money. He used his wealth, knowledge…and skill…to create one of the greatest collections of manuscripts in America.

In 1984, Forbes went head-to-head with Texas billionaire Ross Perot in a high-end bidding war. The price: Forbes paid just over $200,000.00

It turned out to be an excellent investment. The ultimate capitalist knew a good thing when he saw it. The manuscript was an excellent investment and it was sold, after Forbes' death, for almost $3 million!

So you see, being last isn't so bad after all.

Lincoln Wore Glasses

OPERA GLASSES WERE once as common as...well, as common as operas, and just as elaborate!

The first opera glasses were actually little telescopes. There was just one lens and the body was decorated with gems, enamel, ivory and other decorations. (Fancy schmancy!)

> ### 'Tis Better to Give Than To Receive
> Opera glasses were commonly presented as gifts and tributes and it's not uncommon to find inscriptions and dedications engraved on them.

But in 1823, the town that brought us both operas and schnitzels—Vienna—introduced the world to opera glasses, fancy binoculars destined to be the essential fashion accessory for opera buffs.

"Jealousy glasses" offered a different perspective on things. These combination spyware-opera glasses featured a sneaky sideways mirror. They made it possible to discretely observe the action in the audience, as well as the action on the stage.

Opera glasses were an invaluable asset for the well-dressed theater-goer, and it's easy to pick up "standard issue" vintage lorgnettes (opera glasses on a stick) for under $100.

But to collectors, its the eyes *behind* the glasses that make them worth a pretty penny...or, in one case, nearly a half million dollars.

The opera glasses used by Abraham Lincoln at Ford's Theatre on the night of his assassination sold at auction for $424,000.

Andrew Jackson Does Hard Time

WE TALK A lot about the Great Depression of the 1930's, but things were pretty depressing 100 years earlier during the "hard times" of President Andrew Jackson.

Jackson believed that too much of the financial power of the country rested in private hands. Those hands were digging deep into the pockets of Americans and causing prices of goods and services to skyrocket.

To combat the runaway inflation, Jackson issued an order forcing banks and anyone else receiving public money to accept only gold and silver money for the sale of public land.

The immediate result was the tightening of money and the failure of many banks and business. Everyone started hording coins.

"Hard times"…made it tough to do business! So political activists and merchants privately minted "hard time" large-cent-sized copper tokens to take up the slack.

Many hard time tokens were simply advertising pieces. But others combined commerce with politics. They featured satire and propaganda along with their sales messages.

> To avoid charges of counterfeiting, many businesses created hard times tokens with the slogan "Millions for defense NOT ONE CENT for tribute."

"I take the responsibility," says Andrew Jackson, standing in an empty treasure chest, on a famous hard time token.

The value of hard time tokens is determined more by supply and demand than by individual rarity, and even common tokens can sell for up to $100.

Not bad for a coin that's not even worth a penny.

Pin Your Hopes on the President

EVERYBODY LOVES A winner, of course. But in the world of political memorabilia, it's the losers who are winners. Some of the most valuable campaign mementos are the posters, the signs, and especially the pins and buttons from the side that crashed and burned.

Leon says, "I've held on to trinkets from the campaigns of Ralph Nader, Ross Perot, and Michael Dukakis. I've even got a few "Muskie for President" buttons leftover from '72."

They're growing more valuable by the year.

Most people toss their buttons into the trash. It's not an insult. Campaign buttons are meant to be throwaway advertising. But as a result, many of the buttons that survived are likely to have been forgotten in the bottom of a trunk or jewelry box...rather than intentionally preserved with tender, loving care.

History Lesson

Active presidential campaigning and the use of mementos for advertising did not begin until the mid 1800's. One reason for the delay is that it was considered "improper" to openly seek the office of President. After being nominated, candidates stayed at home and awaited the results. (And they say nothing ever changes in politics!)

So just what's the value of gone-but-not-forgotten campaign "swag"?

The biggest winners among the losers are trinkets. There's a particularly large interest in campaign buttons for unsuccessful candidates prior to World War II.

At a recent auction, a tiny 1920 "Cox and Roosevelt" pin brought in over $23,000.

Sometimes, it pays to lose!

WE'RE IN THE MONEY

~ ABOUT COINS ~

"Lack of money is the root of all evil."
~ George Bernard Shaw

"If you want to know what God thinks of money,
just look at the people he gave it to."
~ Dorothy Parker

BEFORE BEANIE BABIES—before baseball cards—before Barbies—there were stamps and coins. Stamps and coins still represent the largest collecting interest in the world. Everyone has seen, held, and used stamps and coins, but few of us know what makes them collectible and valuable. Perhaps you have slipped a valuable silver quarter into a Coke machine or licked a rare stamp to send a letter to a friend. Knowing what to look for can keep those valuable collectibles from being used for soda pop and postage.

The collectible values of both stamps and coins are based upon the economic law of supply and demand. Supply is the number of stamps or coins available to the collector. Demand is the desire to hold, have or own the stamp or coin. The greater the demand, the more valuable an item usually is. The fewer number of items available, (less supply) the greater the value as well.

A collector can easily determine the original supply of stamps and coins by researching the quantities produced in most coin and stamp references.

These references, available at your local library, describe every coin and stamp issued and list the quantity minted or printed. The quantities produced do not necessarily indicate the number available today. Stamps are routinely used and discarded. Coins are taken out of circulation as they become worn (or lost through holes in pant pockets).

But quantity is not necessarily the most important factor in establishing value. It is the supply of desirable stamps and coins that create those rare headlines: "Penny Worth Two Thousand Dollars Found in Attic." The most desirable (and valuable) stamps and coins are usually scarce and in excellent condition.

The same supply and demand rules apply to postage stamps. Generally, unused stamps are more valuable than used stamps. Stamps in superb condition are usually more valuable than stamps in poor condition.

Stamp collectors look for stamps that are well centered and have even, uniform margins. Stamps that are clean and free of tears are more valuable than their dirty, worn counterparts.

Just because a stamp or coin is old does not mean it will be valuable. A coin from the Constantine Period of the Roman Empire, which is about 330-345 AD and is over 1,600 years old, and some types can be purchased from a reputable coin dealer for under $50.00.

This Roman Empire coin is quite interesting, but for many years these coins were sold by the bagful (high supply, but low demand).

Likewise, a full sheet of commemorative stamps from the 1940's is worth little more than the value of the postage. Indeed, dealers pay less than face value for most of these stamps. Even as an entire sheet, these stamps are available in great quantities and there is little demand for them as collectibles, let alone as postage—you would need a pretty large envelope to hold enough postage and send a first class letter.

But before you run off to buy or sell (or appraise) stamps and coins, here are a few tips from the professionals—uh, that would be us.

Do some research on your own. Find a dealer that has a history of fair dealings. Don't rush to buy or sell. Shop around. Get more than one price or offer, and remember to feel out the dealer's knowledge before you make a buying or selling decision. Better yet, consult with an appraiser who specializes in the field.

Some stamps and coins can be found in the form of collections, while others are just accumulations. There is a big difference between a collection and an accumulation. A collection is an organized group of stamps or coins. Collections are usually well-cared for and properly stored and sorted in albums. An accumulation is a batch of coins in a coffee can or a pile of stamps in one big envelope.

The items that make up a collection are almost always in better condition than the items in an accumulation. That means the value of a collection is usually greater than an accumulation containing the same material. So keep you eyes open for good, clean collections of stamps and coins. Happy hunting!!

Dude Looks Like a Lady

A DIME…ONE-tenth of a dollar…was among the first coins authorized by the newly established U.S. mint in 1796.

But do you know the ten-cent piece that's a real "gender bender"? It's got the face of a lady, but it's known by a very masculine name.

Stumped? It's the Mercury dime, released in 1916, and minted in San Francisco, Denver, and Philadelphia. It was in production until FDR died in 1946 and a new design featuring a portrait of the former President was minted.

So what's the gender-bender secret of the Mercury dime?

It's the portrait on the face side of the coin. Adolph A. Weinman, the coin's designer, stated that the obverse figure is a depiction of Lady Liberty wearing a winged cap, symbolizing freedom of thought.

But Americans had other ideas. And they decided to take "freedom of thought" literally. It became commonly accepted that the portrait wasn't Miss Liberty at all. Instead, it was identified as the Roman god who was also known for his winged head and footgear.

"We, the People" dubbed the ten-cent coin, "The Mercury Dime."

The Other Side Of Mercury

There are more American symbols on the reverse of the Mercury dime. Flip it over and you'll find fasces (a bundle of rods wrapped around an ax with a protruding blade) juxtaposed with an olive branch. The images were intended to symbolize authority, preparedness, and peace.

Only 264,000 coins were part of the 1916-D issue of the Mercury dime. They have become among the most sought after (and expensive) coins in American numismatics. One thin dime brought $5,750 at a California auction in 2005.

A Penny Saved

TEACHING KIDS THE value of a dollar...or a pound...was just as tough back in Queen Victoria's day as it is now. In the late 1800's, however, smart parents thought the solution was to make a game of it.

(Could that be the origin of the expression "laughing your way to the bank"?)

Smart toy manufacturers decided to cash in on the idea. They created whimsical mechanical banks. These cleverly designed cast iron wonders put some fun in finance.

And they made kids want to save a penny just to watch the bank in action.

The game started with placing a coin on the bank. The child then pulled a lever or pressed a button to set the game in motion. Presto! The coin would disappear into the base.

The banks came in every size and shape you could think of. There were acrobats, monkeys, lions, and Jonah and the whale. Some were houses and others were buildings.

Other popular banks featured people engaged in an activity...a man shooting a bear in a tree...a boy coaxing a dog to jump through a hoop...an organ grinder and his monkey.

One of the most popular banks was the Humpty Dumpty bank. It featured the painted face of a well-known French mime. Today, Humpty Dumptys can sell for more than $2,000.

You'd need a dozen vintage banks to hold all the pennies it took to buy one of the rarest "coin collectors" that still exists...

It's the politically incorrect "Darky & Watermelon Bank." The coin is kicked like a football into the receptacle. Made by JE Stevens in 1888, it recently brought over $350,000 at auction!

Now that's a collectible with a value you can bank on!

> Here's how *House and Garden Magazine* in, 1930 described the bank action: "When you opened the door a little iron man appeared bearing a tray in his hand. You placed a cent on the tray (if you had one) and closed the door, and the little man stepped back and dropped the penny into a slot inside the house."

Eagles vs. Indians

The penny has been shrinking ... and we don't mean in value.

Large cents—called pennies—were first minted in the U.S. in 1793. The government kept cranking them out until the middle of the 19th Century. At that point, the coins were becoming too expensive to produce.

Congress stepped in. They did what they do best. A little cutting...of cost and size! In 1856, they introduced a smaller, copper coin known as the Eagle Cent (not the Eagle Penny).

The coin was also known as "the Flying Eagle."

The 1856 Flying Eagle cent is one of the few American coins whose value is greater than its rarity. It can be worth more than $2,000!

But the Eagle has *always* been valuable. Even as early as the late 1850s, original mints of Flying Eagles were worth as much as $2, depending on their condition.

So the penny was out and the Eagle was in, but not for long.

Because of design problems, Flying Eagles emerged from the mint weakly struck, especially at the eagle's tail and wingtip. Chief Engraver James B. Longacre was ordered to prepare a new and improved design.

Longacre worked hard to save the endangered bird. He tried several refinements of the design, and as a result 1858 may well have witnessed the striking of more unconventional U.S. cents than any other year.

But the Eagle's days were numbered. In January of 1859, the U.S. Mint replaced it with the Indian Head penny.

A Good Head on Your Penny

YOU'VE PROBABLY HEARD that Indian Head pennies are great collectibles and worth some good money. And that's true…to a degree.

The Indian Head is popular because of its "good looks," not because of its rarity. The obverse of the pretty little copper coin has a lovely Indian princess in a feathered headdress. The word "LIBERTY" is on her headband.

Many citizens believed that the portrait on the front of the coin represented Liberty wearing an Indian headdress, rather than an actual Indian. Legend has it that the model for the Indian Head cent was the designer's daughter Sarah.

The story said that Sarah was present when an Indian delegation was visiting her father's office. One of the chiefs placed a war bonnet on the girl's head and that became the inspiration for her father's design of the coin.

Now, Indian Head pennies are as common as clover. They were minted for half-a-century starting in 1859…and over 1.8 billion Indian Head cents were produced in all before they were replaced by the Lincoln cent in 1909. That's a lot of copper!

> **In the Lab with Leon**
> The new copper coin wasn't all copper. It had about 12% nickel mixed in.

Each year they were in production, the U.S. mint turned out between 8 million and 49 million coins! But in 1877…

Well, let's just say it was a bad year for pennies and a good year for collectors.

Less than one million Indian Head pennies were minted in 1877. That makes 'em rare…and valuable.

An 1877 coin with a good "head" on its shoulders can sell for close to $1,000!

Call a New Jersey Copper!

SOME PEOPLE THINK that the "big money" has always been in New York. Some people are wrong! Americans first started making money in a little town across the river from New York.

In New Jersey.

Okay, it wasn't "big money" at first. It was coins. Lots of coins. Millions of 'em, in fact.

In 1786, New Jersey's Colonial legislature called for three million "coppers." No, it wasn't an authorization for a new police force. The legislature approved the minting of the coins called "New Jersey Coppers" that would ultimately come to be known as "pennies."

> **Impersonating a Copper**
> There are a few very rare lightweight counterfeit New Jersey coppers, but only 3 or 4 examples of most of them exist. The "Serpent Head," was the only mass produced counterfeit. Some of these fakes have sold at auction for more than $500.

The coppers were minted in Morristown, Rahway, and Elizabeth (then known as Elizabethtown), New Jersey, and in Newburg…which is actually in New York!

> **By Any Other Name**
> Despite the fact that we all use the word "penny," the U.S. Mint has never actually minted a coin for which that is the official name.

The obverse (face side) of the coin features a horse's head and plow, with the words Nova Caesarea (Latin for New Jersey). The reverse side has a U.S. shield and what was then a "newly minted" Latin phrase describing the newly minted nation itself.

That's right! New Jersey has the distinction of being the first to use the national motto *e pluribus unum* (one from many).

The Jersey pennies were only minted for a few years, but they're not all that rare. Most are valued at under $100.

But still…that's a 1000% return on your 1-cent investment. Not bad for a penny.

Change for the Better

HERE'S A BRAIN-twister for all you math wizards out there:

How can you pay for a 75-cent candy bar with a one-dollar bill…and get more than 50-cents in return? (This is the kind of "new math" we need to teach the government!)

Need a hint? It's not what you give…it's what's you get.

The trick is in the change. If the mom-and-pop candy storeowner hands you a quarter from the 1960's...or earlier...you've scored "solid gold."

Well, solid silver actually. Quarters were minted in silver through 1964. The following year, the process was changed and new coins contained a thin layer of copper sandwiched between two outer silver layers.

Tricky!

> **Panning for Gold, Edging for Silver**
> Place the coins in a row on their edge and look for beige areas without a brown streak to find silver coins.

The price of silver has been going up, up, up and away, lately. As a matter of fact, when we first wrote the original Betcha on this topic, silver prices were half what they are today!

The rising cost of silver means that the silver in pre-1965 coins is worth three to four times the value of the denomination.

So a silver dime is worth 30 cents, a half-dollar is worth a buck-and-a-half, or more.

And that 1960's quarter you got along with your chocolate bar? It's worth a cool 75-cents, or more!

That sure leaves a good taste in your mouth!

Can't Win For Losing

CAN YOU NAME the U.S. coin that holds three...count 'em 3...first place records, but is still considered a loser?

The coin is:

- The first non-gold dollar of such small size.
- The first U.S coin with a non-circular edge
- The first U.S. coin to picture a real life woman... as opposed to a mythic or symbolic figure.

President Jimmy Carter approved minting the coins on October 10, 1978. That earned them the nicknamed "Carter Quarters" despite their real value. And in 1979, the old Eisenhower dollar was replaced with...

The Susan B. Anthony dollar coin.

757,813,744 Anthony dollars were produced the first year. Ultimately, the United States Mint produced 888,842,452 Susan B.'s for circulation.

But the "Anthony dollar" has never achieved the mythic stature of a Kennedy half, for example. It's never been able to win the hearts and minds of the public...or collectors.

Even original, hot-off-the-1979-presses Susan B.'s are only worth about a buck.

In fact, if you factor in inflation...they may actually be losing value!!!

Die and Die Again

THE YEAR WAS 1955—fast cars, fast women, and a fast minting process that changed the value of a copper cent into solid gold.

There was a problem with the die process for the 1955 Lincoln Cent. The way in which the mint created the image on the coin was flawed. The President's face looked fine, but the face of the coin—the obverse—had a double image of both the date and the legend.

It was kind of like blurred vision.

The result was a mutant...an imperfection...a collectors' dream. It was one of many "double-die" coins produced by the Mint and also one of the most popular.

Words To "Die" For

Die - an engraved metal stamp used for stamping out the design of a coin.

Double die - a coin that shows numbers or letters doubled caused by the coin die having been made with a doubled design on parts of it

Die clash - damage to a coin die that occurs when the top and bottom dies collide without a planchet (blank, unstruck coin) in the press.

Die defect - damage or defect of a coin die.

Die variety - an alteration in the basic design of a coin.

As soon as the error was spotted, the Mint immediately stopped production. But immediately wasn't quick enough. The Mint "freed" the pennies and a few of the flawed Abrahams ended up released into circulation—about 24,000.

So the next time you pay your bar bill and think you're "seeing double" on the penny you put down… Stop! If it's not the drink, it could be a double-die. You could be giving that bartender a tip worth thousands of dollars!

And *nobody's* that good!

Two Eagles Are Better Than One

WANT TO KNOW what makes the value of a gold coin soar like an eagle? It's two eagles…which is exactly what you'll find on the most coveted gold coin ever minted in the United States.

In 1933, 445,000 Double Eagles, a $20 gold coin, were minted. Great coin…bad timing. In January of 1934, FDR pushed through the Gold Reserve Act that outlawed the circulation and private possession of U.S. gold coins.

Gold coins were no longer "legal tender" and had to be exchanged for other forms of currency. People complied…at least most of them…and the gold coins were melted down by the "authorities" in late 1934.

America's Most Wanted

In August 2005, the U.S. Secret Service announced the recovery of ten Double Eagles from the family of Philadelphia jeweler Israel Switt…a man who admitted to selling the first nine Double Eagles recovered a half-century earlier. Currently, the coins are held at Fort Knox under lock and key.

So, if you've got a set of double eagles…someone out there is looking for you too!

The United States Mint presented a pair of Double Eagles to the U.S. National Numismatic Collection. So *technically*…any Double Eagles in circulation should have been returned to the Feds, leaving only the two coins in the collection as "mementos."

But hold on. That's not all, folks. There were dirty doings going on! A number of the Double Eagle coins—no one knows how many—were apparently stolen, possibly by someone very close to the U.S. Mint.

But get this: the theft wasn't discovered until 1944!

Then the Secret Service was on the case, and within the first year of the investigation, seven of the coins were discovered and turned over to federal agents…or seized.

"POST IT" NOTES

~ ABOUT STAMPS ~

There are more than 200 million stamp collectors worldwide

*An estimated 25 million people collect stamps
in the United States alone*

Stamp Love

"PHILATELIST" IS ONE of those ten-dollar words that industry "insiders" like to toss around.

Don't be intimidated. It's just a fancy way of saying "stamp collector." And you can use that knowledge to have some fun at stamp shows.

Sidle up to some stamp snob in your best "rube" voice and ask, "Are you one of them philatelists folks?"

Mr. or Ms. Snob will probably look down a long, judgmental nose at you and answer with a curt "Yes" in response.

The fun is about to begin.

Ask innocently, ""What does that word mean, exactly?' and wait patiently in the silence that inevitably follows. Then, answer the question yourself!

"Golly, I think it comes from the Greek word 'philo' meaning 'love' and 'atelea' meaning 'free from tax.' You see, in ancient Greece, when a message was delivered with a stamp on it, it freed the recipient from paying."

Stamp Facts

There's an old riddle that goes something like this:

What never leaves the corner, but travels the world?

Answer: a postage stamp.

Why do we suggest this?

Frankly, in our opinion, there's no room for snobbery in stamp collecting. BUT, there's always plenty of room for sharing knowledge and info.

Remember: A love of stamps shouldn't override a love for your fellow man (and woman).

Not Until You're Dead

U.S. POSTAGE STAMPS are history with a sticky backing.

Stamps commemorate important events like the signing of the Declaration of Independence, the invention of the light bulb, and the discovery of the cure for polio.

Sometimes stamps celebrate different industries. For example, transportation has been given the "stamp treatment" with illustrations of breakthroughs like the automobile, the steam-driven train, and the airplane.

If you've ever fantasized about having your picture on a postage stamp and joining the ranks of activists, entertainers, athletes, creative artists, sports heroes, musicians, inventors, and world leaders whose famous faces that have been immortalized on stamps, this may take the wind out of your sails...

U.S. Post Office regulations say that **no living people can be featured on a stamp**—except for historic and presidential stamp—and the "dead and gone" must be "gone" for 10 years.

So, if you see your face on a U.S. postage stamp, you're definitely famous, but you're also definitely dead.

HOWEVER...in 2004, the Postal Service *did* approve the creation of stamps with personalized images: like your face!

Self-created stamps are considered 'metered mail.' They're exempt from the regulations for regular stamps.

So go ahead and make a stamp that commemorates YOU. You won't be breaking the law, just bending it a bit.

When Wrong Is Right

IN 1918, WHEN the Curtis Jenny bi-plane was all the rage, the Postmaster General flew into a rage of his own when a mistake was made during the printing process.

> So here's a question for you. With so many Elvis sightings, does the King really, really belong on a US postage stamp?

Congress had just set the rate for airmail postage at 24¢ and authorized the U.S. Post Office to print a red stamp with a blue picture of the popular Curtis Jenny bi-plane.

Good idea…bad execution. When the two million stamps were printed, a small quantity came out with the airplane upside down! (Good enough for government work, as the saying goes.)

According to the Smithsonian Museum, only 100 Inverted Jennys slipped past inspectors at the Bureau of Printing and Engraving and found their way to the public at the end of World War I.

Collectors jumped on the small batch of misprints like Kodiak bears on Alaskan salmon. All 100 instantly became collector's items.

It's generally agreed that only eighty Inverted Jennies exist today. The fate of the remaining 20 stamps remains a mystery.

There's no mystery about the value of this high-flying airmail stamp though: a single Inverted Jenny stamp may sell for $100,000 or more, depending on its condition.

Do not fold, spindle or multiage!

Air Mail's "Big Three"

Perhaps the most famous airmail stamps are the "Zeppelins" These three stamps known by stamp collectors as C-13, C-14, and C-15, became some of the hottest stamp collectibles based on the when they were released. Today, they are still in demand, but the frenzy to acquire them has faded.

Salvage Your Selvage

FEELING SHARP? THEN tackle this brainteaser:

What is it that is part of a stamp, though not part of a stamp, but if missing will make a stamp less valuable?

Give up? The answer is **selvage.**

Not familiar with the term? Then it's time for another "Daniel Webster Moment."

The selvage is the outer, unprinted margin on a sheet of stamps. The selvage may include the plate number, copyright, and other markings.

Selvage itself has no value. But it does ADD VALUE to your stamps. Let's fly to the Middle East for an example…

Got your passport?

If you pull the selvage from a set of three 1948 Israeli stamps you could reduce their value from $4,000.00 to $100.00

Lose three little tabs of paper and you lose $3,900…that's $1,300 per tear!

George Washington Loses to Ben Franklin?

GEORGE WASHINGTON MAY have been the first U.S. president, but someone else beat him out for the honor of "first face" on a U.S. postage stamp. That distinction belongs to Benjamin Franklin.

How come?

Franklin was chosen to appear on the 5-cent stamp in recognition of his role as the first Postmaster General of the U.S. Confederation. (Yup, that's what they called it back then).

The first U.S. postage stamp was issued in 1847, long after both men were pushing up daisies. It cost 5-cents and paid the "passage" for a letter to travel up to 300 miles from the sender. It was also imperforate.

Imperfo-who? It's time to call on Daniel Webster again.

Great Scott!
The Franklin 5-cent stamp and the Washington 10-cent stamp are referred to by collectors as Scott #1 and Scott #2, regarding their place in the philatelists' "bible," the Scott Specialized Catalogue of United States Stamps and Covers.

An imperforate stamp has no little holes around the edges. The holes are called perforations, or "perfs" for short.

The first sheets of stamps didn't nearly tear apart the way today's "models" do. It was necessary for postal clerks to hand-cut the required number of straight-edged stamps from sheets. (Think what *that* would do to waiting time at the post office!)

An unused, mint condition, 5-cent Benjamin Franklin stamp is estimated to be worth over $4,000. BUT…an unused specimen of the second stamp ever issued—the 10-cent George Washington—is valued at over $20,000.

In this case of stamp value, a U.S. President trumps a U.S. Postmaster General!

Free Franklin!

BENJAMIN FRANKLIN WAS a printer, an inventor, and one of the signers of the Declaration of Independence. He was also frugal…it was his "mission."

When he hit the ripe old age (for then!) of 20, Franklin decided to embark on what he called "moral perfection." He created a list of four resolutions to follow. He resolved to become more frugal so that he could save enough money to repay what he owed to others.

So Franklin had one eye on the mail and one eye on his bottom line. And the "father" of the future U.S. postal system took advantage of a nice "perk" while serving as postmaster of the American colonies.

He enjoyed a "franking privilege." To send his missives on their way, all Franklin had to do was sign his name on an envelope and write the word "free."

No fuss…no muss…and no stamp.

Now frugal Franklin may have been tight with a buck, but he was very generous with his political protests. And instead of singing his mail "B. Franklin, Free"…the sneaky devil wrote,

"B. Free Franklin"

IT WAS A clever subliminal message broadcasting his commitment to gaining freedom and independence from the

Abuse of the Franking Privilege

Not unlike some slimy politicians of today, there are stories of 19th century Congressman who abused the system and squandered tax dollars. Some were accused of shipping their laundry home using the franking privilege.

The greatest abuse however, was reported to have been conducted by a Pennsylvania Senator who wrote his name on the bridle of his horse and had it shipped back to his home in Pennsylvania, at taxpayer's expense.

English government. Recently this special "protest signature frank" sold for over $18,000.

The Franklin Privilege still exists today. You can see examples of it when you receive official mail from your Congressman or Senator.

And you thought that wigged-out old trickster just fooled around with kites!

Z-Grill is Ze Best

THE GEORGE FOREMAN grill may offer you a better burger, but if you're a stamp fan, it's all about the "z-grill."

Before we get to "Z," however, let's start at "A"…the beginning…and a visit with Leon's dictionary.

Defining Terms

A **stamp grill** is a type of embossing on stamps. Like a lot of great ideas, it was created to try to foil criminal activities.

What do you do with a nation that's recovering from a Civil War and a federal government that's looking for ways to fund rebuilding efforts?

Today, they raise taxes, but in 1860, a smart fellow named Charles Steel figured that if the U.S. Postal Service **embossed** stamps, it would make postal cancellations harder to remove. If cancellations couldn't be removed, the stamps couldn't be re-used; so more stamps would have to be purchased.

And that meant more money, more money, and more money for the cash-poor government.

Most people who hear this story say, "That's dumb!"… but it took the government a little longer to come to that conclusion. Still, shortly after the stamp embossing program was instituted, it was pulled.

Few were minted…and fewer remain. In fact, there are only two "z grill" stamps known to exist. One is at the New York Public Library, and the Mystic Stamp Company owns the other.

As for value…the "holy grail" of stamps has been appraised at $2.5 million.

In fact, one California collector traded a block of four 1918 stamps valued at $3 million for a single "Z Grill" stamp. The "Z" completed the collector's 300-stamp collection representing every 19th-century U.S. postage stamp ever made.

Talk about A-Z!!!

Mr. Zip-a-dee-do-dah

THE U.S. POST Office was not always the model of efficiency it is today. It wasn't until 1963 that the Zonal Improvement Plan (ZIP) was instituted.

Quit Your Moaning!

THE USPS IS doing a helluva job, even if you don't realize it. It has 38,000 post offices, 200,000 vehicles, 15,000 daily flights and 729,000 career employees whose only goal is to deliver 200 billion pieces of mail each year through rain and snow and dark of night. (Don't forget to say thank you!)

So what's the big deal about a zip code?

In the pre-ZIP world, envelopes were manually sorted, which was much slower and was becoming more expensive by the year. The creation of ZIP codes allowed electronic processing and delivery of mail at a price the Federal government found very attractive.

The zip code assigned a specific code to every city, town, village, and hamlet in the U.S. It reduced misdirected mail and improved service.

The Post Office was in love with ZIP. Their challenge: how to "turn on" the American public?

The job fell to a little cartoon character named "Mr. Zip."

The wide-eyed Mr. Zip is a cheery mail carrier all decked out in his blue hat and uniform. He can be spotted in the margins ('selvage') of many stamps above the slogan "Use Zip Code."

Not only is Mr. Zip popular with his fellow letter carriers, but collectors love him, too. Stamps with Mr. Zip fetch a premium price.

Stamp Sales Go Into Orbit

DURING THE KENNEDY years, the space race was in full swing and America had its eyes on the stars…literally!

Do you know the 1962 event that made history twice?

On February 20th, at 2:43 p.m., astronaut John Glenn made his historic splash down in the Atlantic after orbiting the Earth four times aboard the Mercury Friendship 7. (What a view!)

It was one small splash for man… And one giant splash for the post office: As soon as Glenn was safely aboard his recovery ship, a 4-cent stamp commemorating the successful mission was issued.

In a "covert operation," the special stamp had been secretly printed. Then it was distributed and held at post offices around the country until the "thumbs up" was given.

There's only one word to describe what happened when the post office issued its surprise announcement regarding the Glenn commemorative stamp…

STAMP-EDE!

People flooded post offices around the country in a Space Age buying frenzy that had never been seen before. When the day was over, more than 10 million "Project Mercury" stamps were available to the public, any many of these were scooped up by speculating stamp collectors.

Today, those stamps sell for about the same price as the issue price, four cents.

ADS & ADVERTISING: BATTLE OF THE BRANDS

~ ABOUT AMERICA'S FAVORITE PRODUCTS ~

"Many a small thing has been made large
by the right kind of advertising."
~ *A Connecticut Yankee in King Arthur's Court*, Mark Twain

IT'S A FUNNY thing. Advertising is not really a product, like furniture or glass; it's telling something about a product. It's kind of like ephemera, a big word that simply means throwaway paper. These "items" aren't produced to be kept or enjoyed, but simply to be consumed and then thrown away. Advertisements point to some item, product, or service that is meant to be consumed, kept, or enjoyed.

What we find so amazing about old advertising, signs, and displays is that this advertising ephemera is worth more than the product it promoted. You wouldn't think of keeping an advertisement from today's newspaper as a symbol of art, graphic design, or beauty, but some people don't bat an eyelash about spending big bucks on a 100 year old country store tin that sold coffee, a cardboard display with the price of today's eggs, or a paper fan advertising the virtues of a specific line of clothing.

Part of this perception of value stems from a negative reaction to modern mass communication, like television, video, and Internet, and part from the nostalgic tug of certain by-gone or popular products. Years ago, advertisers of any good or service had to rely upon either word of mouth or a catchy, colorful, and stylish container to hawk their ware. The better the design, the brighter the color, and the more identifiable the brand, the more successful the product (and the more collectible it becomes today).

Another alternative was to offer free or low priced premiums, often with the same name or logo to identify and promote the goods. These can range from genuine "antiques"-like ceramic bowls, plates, or crockery, to oddities like rubber tire ashtrays or glass paperweights. All of these items now command serious attention and probably their own "collector's club."

The variety and scope of this category is simply amazing. Almost anything ever produced as advertising either here or abroad now has a following. People collect by brand name, by product type, by city or region, and often by sub-category, like printer, manufacturer, or original artist.

Lest we forget, the biggest category is probably signage—the paper, wood, or metal signs that identify a certain product, store, or tradesman. These can range from old gas station pole tops with the Texaco Star to 2 feet-long figural pipes that indicated a smoke or tobacco shop. I think the best just might be the old wood signs that say "ANTIQUES." (How old can they be?)

Remember, this stuff wasn't meant to be used—except as advertising. Just imagine what they would have done if they knew people would save it? Kind of strange, isn't it?

Super Sipper

MORE THAN 95 million American viewers tune in to the annual Super Bowl. Internationally, nearly a billion sports fans are also rooting for their favorites to "hold that line."

Some years, the battle between the commercial brands on the screen is more exciting than the battle between the football teams on the field. And one "team" you can always expect to see at the Super Bowl is soda pop advertising.

The odds-on favorite to win: America's #1 soft drink, Coca Cola. Coke ads are as much a part of the Super Bowl as the national anthem!

Coca Cola advertising has been around for more than 100 years. And people have been collecting Coke memorabilia—signs, calendars, and displays—for just as long!

One of the most popular collectibles is a serving tray. At your local mall, you may have seen reproductions featuring the red Coca Cola logo and a picture of an attractive girl.

But the real "beauty" is the tray, not the girl. The tray with the highest value date back to the 1880's. That's when Coca Cola was born to Dr. John S. Pemberton in his Atlanta, Georgia laboratory.

Coke products can sure be valuable, particularly those from the early part of the 20th century, but what about their logo? The Coca-Cola trademark is reportedly worth over $25 billion. That's a lot of soft drinks!

There are nearly 5,000 people who consider themselves Coke Collectors. Their web site is www.cocacolaclub.org. If you're ever in Atlanta, stop by the World of Coca Cola. It has over 1,200 different pieces of memorabilia and advertising collectibles. If you've got something they don't have, take heart. Coke wants it. It may not be worth $25 billion, but it might get you a whole lot of Coke.

Now don't rush off to your computer and try to Google "Coke 1880." You'll come up empty-handed. The name "Coke" wasn't used until the 1940's.

Coke collectibles from the 1940's and 1950's are popular and sometimes pricey, but the BIG money goes to a 13"x 19" embossed, oval tin tray made in 1926. It sold for over $17,000.00.

Take that, Pepsi!

No Soap Radio...COKE Radio

WHEN YOU'VE WORKED up a thirst, there's no more welcoming site than a soda pop machine. Drop in a few coins and bingo: icy cold bubbly sweetness that tastes like the nectar of the gods!

Perhaps it's the memory of that refreshing experience that makes soda pop collectibles so appealing. And you know what's interesting...satisfying your hunger for soda pop collectibles is a lot like satisfying your thirst…the brand doesn't really matter!

Except when it comes to the mother (and father) of all soda pop collectibles—Coca Cola.

Some early Coca Cola memorabilia is worth more than most people realize. With so many reproductions on the market, it's easy to get the mistaken impression that Coca Cola items are common. But the truth is that there are some "crazy" prices being paid for old and unusual advertising items with the Coca Cola logo.

One of our favorites is the trademark Coca cola bottle that's also a radio. It's authentic, and complete with bottle cap and logo. But this amazing collectible is also an old-fashioned 24" tube radio.

The Coca Cola bottle is the same shape as a regular Coke bottle. The top clear section is the on/volume control and the clear base is the tuning control. The dark section separates so that batteries can be inserted.

It was meant to function as a real receiver. And we're not the only ones who are "sweet" on it. People all over the world are snapping them up.

Have a Coke radio and a smile!

A Winning Formula

IF A PLUCKY druggist hadn't been dedicated, one of America's most popular cola-flavored soda syrups might have simply "fizzled out."

It was trial and error before Caleb Bradham formulated "the taste that beats the others cold" at his drugstore in 1893. He named it after himself—"Brad's Drink"—and said, that it was a cure for dyspepsia.

Now, we're not doctors. And we don't play them on radio. But our diagnosis of this claim is that it's completely false!

It was a cure for thirst, however, and Caleb's sweet cola ultimately found its audience.

Two years later, he found its name. In 1898, Caleb purchased the name "Pep Cola" for $100. He then changed the name of his new drink from Brad's Cola to Pepsi-Cola.

In his first three months, Caleb sold 2008 gallons of Pepsi-Cola syrup. Sweet! But not for long.

After the end of World War I, Bradham bought large amounts of sugar as a hedge against increased price levels. Bad move. By 1920, sugar prices had dropped to a low of three cents a pound, and by 1923, bankruptcy was declared. Caleb Bradham returned to his pharmacy...and faded into obscurity.

But Pepsi lived on. The company's trademark and assets sold at auction for $30,000. The new owner, Roy C. Megargel, was only able to keep Pepsi in the black until 1931 when it again went into bankruptcy.

Enter Charles G. Guth. Guth had an axe to grind with the folks at Coca Cola because they had 'done him wrong' over a sugar deal when he was at Loft's Candy. For spite, he bought Pepsi for $10,500 as a rival to Coca Cola.

He adjusted the syrup formula in his soda and modified the bottle itself, too. In 1931, he introduced a 12-ounce bottle at a 6 ounce price. By 1936, his innovation had created a two million dollar operating profit for Guth and revitalized the Pepsi company for years to come.

Times change...tastes change...and America's love affair with Pepsi just keeps going on and on. Vintage Pepsi bottles are popular collectibles which sell for $10 to $20.

And some neon clocks with the bright red, white, and blue Pepsi logo can bring over $2,000.

So when you want a collectible with historic significance and worldwide appeal...say "Pepsi, please!"

Mmmm, Mmmm, Collectible!

INTRODUCING TWO OF the advertising world's most popular pitch-men...actually pitch "twins"...

They are the rosy-checked children known as "The Campbell Kids."

Grace Drayton, a popular illustrator of her day, created the soup tots in 1904. She introduced the little Campbells in a series of trolley car advertisements that were aimed at homemaker moms.

No mother could resist!

But it wasn't just the kids. Campbell's offered 21 varieties of "goodness in a can," each selling for just a dime.

Like spooky little "Portrait of Dorian Gray" clones, the twins never aged. They remained young and freckle-faced in magazine and newspaper ads.

And when the world discovered television, so did the Campbell kids. They made regular TV "appearances" for decades.

Always in fashion and never out of style, in 1990, the Campbell Kids appeared in a commercial singing a rap song about the benefits of their fine soups. It marked the first time since 1958 that the Campbell Soup Twin voices had been heard.

In 1998, Campbell's slogan changed to "Good for the Body, Good for the Soul." The twins also got an extreme makeover. They entered the 21st Century with slimmed down bodies to reflect America's growing health consciousness.

Kids and grown-up kids love the Campbell Kids, and as a result, they have become cherished (and high-priced) collectibles—as figurines, lapel pins, salt and pepper shakes, cookie jars, and toys. A printed, 10" fabric doll from the 50's sells for about $100, while an older version from 1928 lists for up to $400. Not interested in dolls? Then what about the 1920's tin sign that looks like an American flag made out of soup cans? An original sells for $46,000. It seems that only 5 were made. (If you've got one, check it out. We'll bet you $100 it's a reproduction.

The Candy Man

IF YOU CAN guess the name of this "sweet" guy, we've got a kiss for you!

He was a native of Pennsylvania.

He started as an apprentice ice cream maker.

He suffered two major business failures but went on to become one of the world's best-known candy makers.

In 1883, he established the Lancaster Caramel Company but got bitten by the "chocolate bug" and sold his caramel biz for $1 million in 1900.

It took this candy-making pro three years to move his dream forward. In 1903, he was finally able to obtain the large supplies of fresh milk he needed to perfect and produce fine milk chocolate.

Awash in milk, he began construction on what was to become the world's largest chocolate manufacturing plant. It would also be known as the birthplace of "chocolate kisses."

Who is the candy man? It's Milton S. Hershey, the founder of Hershey's Chocolate.

And today, more than 100 years after Milton made magic, his chocolate is still making its way into our mouths, hearts, and minds. Chocolate has been proven to stimulate the release of endorphins, the brain's "feel good" chemical. And a substance in chocolate called phenylethylamine is believed to trigger feelings similar to "falling in love."

We're in love all right…with chocolate!

And we're not the only ones. Folks gobble up Hershey's collectibles as passionately as they devour the company's signature kisses and candy bars. Vintage tins, magazine ads, and even candy wrappers have found their way into the hands of private collectors and public museums.

Hershey built a model town for his employees. The chocolate candy kingdom included comfortable homes, an inexpensive public transportation system, a quality public school system, and extensive recreational and cultural opportunities. But even that wasn't enough for this exceptional entrepreneur.

In 1907, Hershey added an amusement park. Before long, thousands of out-of-town visitors were coming regularly to visit Hershey, Pennsylvania, now known as "the sweetest place on earth." It's a family great trip--take the chocolate tour and ride the coasters!

Rhyme Time

DOES THIS BRING back any memories? If it does…your age is showing (but your whiskers probably aren't).

What well-known soap
Could shave your chin
And leave you with a hairless grin?

It advertised in '26

With roadside signs on top of sticks.

...Burma Shave!

Burma Shave was revolutionary...a *brushless* shaving soap that could be slathered onto the face by hand.

Remarkable!

Even more remarkable were the Burma Shave signs that dotted the nation's highways and byways for nearly 40 years. The familiar white on red signs, grouped by fours, fives and sixes, were as much a part of a family trip as the kids asking "Are we there yet?"

The Burma Shave company sponsored an annual contest for people to submit the rhymes with winners receiving a $100 prize. (Sure beats paying a copywriter!) Some contests received over 50,000 entries.

At the height of their popularity, there were 7,000 Burma-Shave signs stretching across the country.

Burma Shave ads first appeared in 1926, when Americans were taking leisurely drives on country roads. By the 1950's, however, the "need for speed" meant faster cars and faster speeds...and no time to read.

In 1963, the American Safety Razor company bought out Burma Shave and the last ads disappeared from the road.

As time goes by,

And memories cave,

We wont' forget you

...Burma Shave!

AMERICANA: THREE CHEERS FOR THE RED, WHITE & BLUE

"The true meaning of America, you ask? It's in a Texas rodeo, in a policeman's badge, in the sound of laughing children, in a political rally, in a newspaper... In all these things, and many more, you'll find America. In all these things, you'll find freedom. And freedom is what America means to the world. And to me."
~ Audie Murphy

Americana: Is There Such a Thing?

EACH JANUARY, NEW York and other major cities vie for customers and big bucks at their annual Americana auctions. These are supposedly different from other auctions during the year in that they consist of specifically American made or consumed goods.

That limits the field somewhat, since most of everything made today is manufactured in the Far East, although it is consumed in America. To be a purist, Americana items are items that were usually handmade, or at least included a hand process, here in our country to be consumed by our own people. They are antique (maybe a hundred years old or more) and have a definite flavor (like apple pie). They often are important to our own history or the history of American craftsmanship.

Americana includes folk art (the whims and whimsicals of the common people), utilitarian and yet beautiful products, and things that make us distinct from every other country. English porcelain, although made for export to America, would only be allowed in this category if the decoration were specifically American, i.e. George Washington riding his horse. An English teapot, even though bought at Bloomingdales in 1920, would not work.

This field can become very selective. Quilts and samplers, Windsor chairs in green paint (even though Windsor is an English term), Philadelphia formal chests, and carved wooden eagles seem to be the norm. It can also degenerate into anything one wants to sell, like milk glass, Rose Medallion, and reproduction posters of Uncle Sam wanting YOU (notice the finger).

The more selective the selector, the higher the stakes! That's why it's cool. Where and when else can you see a tea table sell for over a million? How about a Baltimore album quilt for nearly $50,000? Maybe a decorated jug for $90,000? Why in 2006 the total amount for Sotheby's Americana auction was almost $25 million.

Whether it's a pair of watercolor portraits by an itinerant 18th century artist or a piece of silver made by Paul Revere, Americana is hot. That's why it's become a catchword and used whenever one wants to impress or provoke.

Fortunately it's not all big bucks. There's a lot of stuff that's just as "nice," almost as interesting, and not quite so pricey. That's the stuff left for you and I AND our Americana is no less significant than theirs. That's why it's fun. After all…this is America!

Face Time

PRIOR TO WORLD War I, there was another battle of major proportions going on. It was the war on whiskers…and the whiskers were winning.

Badly made and tough to keep sharp, razors were crude in those days. The safety razor hadn't been invented yet. Every morning, men were taking their lives into their own hands with their razors.

The only 'safe haven' for a close shave was the barbershop. But there was a problem. The razors may have been better, but the hygiene was for the birds.

In order to protect themselves from the dreaded "barber's itch," men would purchase a personal shaving mug. The mugs usually had the owner's name on it…sometimes in gold script.

Some had illustrations that would depict a fraternal organization, a hobby, or possibly a picture of what the owner did for a living.

Art? No…necessity.

Not everybody could read or write their own name, so the pictures told the story.

We've been trying to find a rare one, ourselves. Unfortunately, much as we've searched, we've never been able to find a shaving mug with two handsome guys doing a radio program.

Let us know if you spot one, okay?

> **Occupational Therapy**
> Mugs that depicted tradesmen and men at work were known as occupational mugs. Rare ones can bring over $500.
>
> Two hot shaving mugs topics are: Masonic and baseball.

Powder Horns Are Powder Kegs

THERE'S NEVER BEEN a shortage of interest in military artifacts. You can choose from weaponry such as rifles and pistols or collect gear including saddlebags and water canteens.

And, of course, military apparel is popular, as well as affordable, for collectors.

For new collectors, "mining" recent conflicts can produce wonderful collectibles. You can invest in them without having to break the bank. But for the "big guns" in military memorabilia, no arsenal of collectibles would be complete without…

Powder horns.

Powder horns are exactly what the name suggests. They're hollowed animal horns used to carry gunpowder. They give some collectors the biggest bang and can command the biggest bucks at auctions.

People collect powder horns for their elaborate carvings and intricate depictions of battle scenes and landscapes. But it's where they were made and who owned them that define their value.

This 'who' and 'where' of an item is know as its 'provenance.'

What's Hot Tip:

Civil War artifacts are perhaps the most desired group of military collectibles. The number of Civil War collectors continues to increase, and the supply of Civil War artifacts continues to decrease. This supply and demand effect, has driven the price of these popular collectibles skyward.

If these increasing prices have kept you from becoming a Civil War collector, try another war. World War II, the Korean War and Vietnam-era artifacts are becoming very popular.

Find items that reflect your interest. Autographs of generals, military photographs, weapons, uniforms, and war effort posters are great places to start.

Provenance, as you may have read in another section of this book, refers to the *evidence of the history of the ownership* of an item. When a powder horn's provenance can show that it was present at specific battles or used by well-known military men, the value really "shoots" up.

Take, for example, a powder horn from the French and Indian Wars, owned and carried by Jabez Johnson. The horn contained a variety of inscribed dates and locations, including a reference to its creation— "Horn Made at Number Four, May the 19th, 1757."

The Johnson horn sold for $34,000. But it takes second place to the relic used by Captain David Baldwin. That piece holds the record for most valuable powder horn sold at auction: $52,800, to be exact.

Now that's something to trumpet about!

Warming Up to Warming Pans

WARMING PANS HAVE been around for centuries. They were a popular item long before restaurants used them to keep meals piping hot for their patrons.

Back in the 18th and 19th Century, keeping your food warm wasn't half as big a deal as keeping yourself warm! So antique warming pans weren't found in the kitchen. They were found in the bedroom.

They were known as 'bed warmers.' It consisted of a brass pan with a hinged lid, and a long 4-foot wooden handle.

Some were simple and some were elaborately engraved. They were all filled with coals from the fireplace and slipped between the sheets to warm the bed linen and the bed.

Warming pans were routinely sold in country stores. They were advertised as being suitable for women who liked to stay in a warm bed. (Apparently the gents of the period were of a heartier stock.)

Bed warmers are fairly common as collectibles. Most sell for between two and three hundred dollars. But a fancy-schmancy warming pan, with lots of ornately tooled metal, can "heat up" at auction and fetch a good price.

So turn down the thermostat and heat up the bed warmers. Hot stuff!

The High Cost of Common Sense

IT'S SAID THAT "common sense" isn't so common.

We agree. First editions of Thomas Paine's "revolutionary" 1776 classic aren't easy to come by. And "Common Sense" is as rare at auctions as it is in real life.

It was "Common Sense" that got the colonists all stirred up with Paine's musings on taxation without representation and how a new, free nation might be formed.

Soon it was party time. No, not a book signing party… A tea party…The Boston Tea Party, to be precise.

The tea got tossed, but not the book. First editions, when they're spotted, can bring a well over $200,000.

But even non-first editions are collectible, and not quite as rare. And don't underestimate the worth of those later printings. They have value, too.

In 2005, Bryn Mawr businessman Jay Snider's received $156,000 for a volume of nine Revolutionary and early federal pamphlets, including Thomas Paine's "Common Sense."

Apparently good sense has its price.

Found Treasures

THE NAME MAY seem like B.S., but a collection of "tramp art" is no bum steer.

Tramp art is a popular "Folk Art" that runs the gamut from "plain and simple" to eye-poppingly complex. The genre includes everything from jewelry boxes to picture frames. There is even tramp art furniture.

To be truly "tramp," the pieces must be made out of tiny scraps of throw-away wood. Most pieces are unsigned and undated, and that adds to the mystique that surrounds them.

Tramp art dates back to the Civil War.

In those days, the artists were soldiers, rather than hobos. Men in uniform, far from home and without money, couldn't find proper art supplies. But they still wanted to make things like gifts for wives, toys for the kiddies, or something special for "ma."

So they used what they *could* find. Like a cheese box, a fruit crate, or a cigar box. Nothing became something as trash was transformed into art with nothing more than imagination, skill, and a pocketknife.

Some tramp-art objects were made as a way for men to pass the time while serving jail sentences for nonviolent crimes like public intoxication.

During the Great Depression, itinerant rural artists and men without work became tramp artists. They chip-carved and glued scraps so they could scratch out a meager living…feed their families…or buy another pack of smokes…kind of like the *Grapes of Wrath*.

Prosperity arrived and tramp art began to disappear in the 1950's. What's rare is valuable, and so the prices for the 'disappearing art' started to soar.

A mirror from 1911 recently sold for $3000 and a sewing box fetched over $1300. And believe it or not, the stuff is so hot that modern plastic reproductions are being sold in upscale magazines.

Crazy!

The Nitty Gritty on Ritty

HERE'S A THROWBACK from the old days, "Ring me up, please."

It's not the "please" that's a leftover from kinder, gentler times. Not at all. It's the "Ring me up" part that's so 19th Century!

At that time, James Ritty ran a bar in Dayton, Ohio—the Pony House—and didn't trust the people who worked for him. He was desperately trying to figure out a way to keep track of sales.

Then in 1878, while traveling on a steamship touring the Atlantic, he heard bells…literally and figuratively.

Ritty became intrigued by a mechanism that counted and sounded the number of times the ship's propeller went around. It gave him an idea for a mechanical device that would record cash transactions and let him known when a sale was made.

Five years later, Ritty and his partner John Birch received a patent for inventing the cash register. It was nicknamed the "Incorruptible Cashier" and became the first working, mechanical cash register.

Ritty died in 1918. But his cash register concept lived on…as did his bar. From 1882 until 1967, it kept going strong by "cashing in" on America's love of alcohol even during Prohibition.

Collectible Household Items

THIS MAY BE the one collectible field that is definitely driven by the grocery store. Not the stuff down the aisles, behind the meat counter, or in refrigerated freezers, but the magazines at the entrance of the cashier lanes. You know what I mean, *Ladies Home Journal*, Martha Stewart *Living*, *Country Living*, Victorian Living, Living in the South, Living in the North, Barely Living, Living Without A Clue, etc.

These magazines become the breeding grounds for "the look." That look is always found in a famous someone's home, usually the kitchen. It's found on the walls, on the counters, hanging from the rafters, piled one upon the other, stored in closets, and even in the bathroom. Along with the look comes advice on where to buy it, how to distress it, and where to pick it up extra cheap at the local flea market.

The look must change, every once in a while, not just to get rid of the dust, but to sell more magazines. Country is in one day, out the next. Victorian comes along and then Shabby Chic (or is it Crappy Shtick). The look is the style we live with. It's what our parents had and what our grandparents decided to throw away. Whatever's on the menu, we'll take.

We love it because it's worn. It's useable. It's comfortable.

That's why this section could include anything—and it does. Everything from glass to furniture, toys to clocks, gadgets to gizmos. Household items are the mundane and the magnificent, the everyday and the eclectic; things like sad irons to iron the clothes (you'll see why they call them sad), turn the crank coffee grinders to grind the beans (find out why electric is so much better), and spatulas with green wooden handles to turn the flapjacks (in a cast iron Griswold griddle).

What house doesn't have one piece of Depression glass, ceramic mixing bowl, or kitchen utensil that came from a previous home or a relative's attic? Whether it be a rolling pin, hanging fruit scale, or a glass kerosene lamp, this is the stuff we decorate with, enjoy, and sometimes pass on to our kids—"have an heirloom from mom". We may change colors, wallpaper, window treatments, sofas and TVs, but this stuff stays (until the annual neighborhood garage sale).

So even though Martha or Rosie or Brett or the latest guru offers their special "look," be forewarned that good, collectible, older household items are always IN no matter what they say. Just wait a couple of months and you'll see it in another version in the same magazine.

HIGHBOYS AND FOOTSTOOLS AND CHAIRS, OH MY!

~ ABOUT FURNITURE ~

THE BEGINNING OF serious thought about furniture was when Plato contemplated the essence of a chair (at least we think he did). His results were that a chair had a back (to rest your back), a seat (to rest your seat), and legs (to rest your legs). We now call that function (what a chair is used for). That part was easy, and they've been making them that way for a heck of a long time.

The other element, one he didn't really comment on, was that a piece of furniture also has form—or "looks." A chair needs a physical body or frame to operate as a chair. It has an appearance, a style, and a distinctive shape that makes it different from other chairs that have the same function. (Is this getting too difficult?)

Certain pieces of furniture just have a better form. They are pretty and they please the eye. People enjoy looking at them and they would much prefer having something that looks like it belongs rather than something that doesn't look like it does.

These pieces become more popular. The people that make them sell more furniture. They become rich and famous. The prices of their furniture begin to rise. It becomes a status symbol to have one of their pieces. The prices continue to rise. They and their furniture become a household name—at least in the rich houses.

Time passes. Someone else comes on the scene. They make the same piece of furniture (function) but in a new and daring style (form). People forget the old. It looks tired and worn out. They want the new. It has better lines, less (or more) carvings, different wood, and creative decorations or embellishments. These new makers become popular. New furniture maker becomes rich, as his or her prices go up.

Pity the previous furniture maker; no one wants those pieces. They are placed in the attic or given to kids going to college. They are painted over-often in white paint. They are even sold at garage sales and flea markets. The furniture still does what it was made to do (seat, eat, store) but anyone "in the know" wouldn't be caught with it in his or her house.

Time passes. More time passes. A lot of time passes. People are tired of all the new forms. What haven't the furniture makers tried? Let's start over. Let's go back to a previously used shape, they think. Why not copy an older style? We could even reproduce the exact form; give it a new look. Maybe add a new curve or twist. Better yet, people don't remember that design. (It's never been in their house.) They might actually like it. We could create a whole new line. We could even bring back the old pieces (if we could find them). Shine them up. Wax their frames. Tighten the joints. Extol their virtues.

Why shouldn't a piece 100 years old be popular? It still has function-just as it did before. It still has form-and what once was pleasing can still be pleasing. The only thing it doesn't have is a high price tag. No one will want that.

I've got an idea. Let's call it an antique. Let's give the original style a name, maybe one after the original maker. We can get the people in the trade, like interior decorators and home magazine writers, to talk it up. We can open little shops that sell only these used (old) pieces. Prices will rise. We'll become rich!

But what if the people get tired of that form? What if they want a different one?

No problem. We'll take another old style. We'll give it a name. We market the heck out of it. People on the cutting edge of fashion will buy it. The little shops will sell it. Prices will rise. We'll become rich!

Thank God we forgot about Plato! After all, a chair is only a chair.

New Names for The New World

MOST ANTIQUE FURNITURE styles are named for their makers. Some are named to honor the monarchs who sat on the throne when the furniture was designed.

Think Louis IX or Victorian or Georgian, for example.

Some honor! Most of the royals would have *hated* a lot of the pieces designed in their "name." Furniture designs were too avant garde for the old guard.

In America, where there was no royal family to please, furniture makers took another route. Instead of being name for people, American furniture was named for periods of history…

Colonial, Pilgrim, and Federal.

Some people say that the inhabitants at 1600 Pennsylvania Avenue are America's monarchs. But the President is only in office for 4 years…8 if he does a good job. And that's too small a "window" of time for a furniture style to be created and take hold.

Besides…who would want to say their furniture is in the "Bush style"? It would sound more like something from the Australian outback!

But don't worry. American presidents may be gone, but their names live on.

We've got JFK Airport, the George Washington Bridge, the Hoover Dam… And at least two former US presidents have species named after them. A deer, an elk and a lion are named after Theodore Roosevelt, while Abraham Lincoln has a wasp and a rose in his name.

Old Presidents never die. They just get their names attached to things.

If There Were A Mount Rushmore For Furniture

IF YOU WANT to be "in the know'" when it comes to furniture styles, there are three men we want you to meet.

Their names are synonymous with great ideas, distinct styles, and period furniture. And although all three styles were developed in England, the names of the men who created them are as familiar to Americans as apple pie.

First comes Chippendale. Not the cute little chipmunks of Disney fame or the tuxedo clad male dancer. This is the stately, London cabinet-maker Thomas Chippendale.

Chippendale's name is emphatically identified with the extensive variety of chair types that he developed. He worked in every imaginable design, from geometrical to Chinese. He incorporated lattice, as well as sumptuously carved and interlaced forms in his work.

Next on the list is George Hepplewhite. His style is characterized by painted or inlaid decoration and distinctive details such as slender, tapering legs and the spade foot.

Rounding out the trio is Thomas Sheraton, whose style is marked by a graceful delicacy and simplicity, emphasis on straight, vertical lines, and a preference for inlay decoration, reeded legs, and classical motifs.

Those who can, do. And sometimes they also teach!

In addition to creating exquisite pieces that are found in every great museum of the world, each of these craftsmen developed handbooks that influenced the world of furniture for generations.

Rocking the White House

MORE THAN ONE American President has had to face rocky times during his career. However, two men who called 1600 Pennsylvania Avenue home will be as remembered for their rocking chairs as for their rocky administrations.

While the kids were rockin' and rollin', John F. Kennedy was just rocking...a lot.

A simple oak porch rocker with arms helped ease the persistent pain in the JFK's back. The one he used sold at auction in 1996 for $442,000.

Lincoln is also known for a rocking chair...

A Lincoln rocker is a high back rocker, usually with a mahogany frame. It is often upholstered or may have a cane back and seat. It has distinctive "swan neck" arms. Rumor has it that this was *not* the President's favorite seat.

Mrs. Lincoln probably wasn't crazy about it either. It was the chair in which he was sitting on April 14th, 1965, the night he was assassinated at Ford's Theatre.

Even though it was associated with a national tragedy, the Lincoln rocker's scrolled arms and upholstered back style remained quite popular. There are quite a few of them around. You may even have one in your home.

They sell for about $200.

> After the assassination, the original Lincoln rocker was confiscated by the War Department to be used as evidence during the trial of the conspirators. In 1866, the rocker was given to the Smithsonian where it remained in storage.
>
> In 1921, a member of the Ford Theatre family asked the government for custody of the rocker. The government complied. The theatre Fords sold the chair at auction to another Ford...a member of the automotive Ford family...for $2,400. Today the chair can be found in the Henry Ford Museum in Dearborn, Michigan.

Rebirth of a Renaissance

VIRTUALLY ALL FURNITURE produced in America from the mid- to the late-19th Century was a revival of one sort or another. First came Gothic, then Rococo, and finally Renaissance Revival.

This Renaissance period was from 1840-1890. During the revival, furniture makers copied the style of the real Renaissance craftsmen from a few centuries before.

They re-embraced straight lines, columns, pediments, busts, medallions, and bronze mounts. The pieces were massive, imposing, and usually made out of rosewood or walnut.

The Wooton Patent Desk is a prime example of Renaissance Revival.

Huge and ornate, the central section of the Wooten desk had two doors that open to the side with rows and rows of cubbyholes and filing slots.

Important names in the American Renaissance of the elaborate European style included Herter and Jeliff. At the top of the list was a Midwestern furniture company...Berkey & Gay.

Berkey & Gay's immense bedroom sets cemented the reputation of the

Grand Rapids factories. They became the go-to manufacturers of "chamber suites," as they were known.

The inevitable end came from two different directions, the desire to return to simplicity and the resurgence of interest in American heritage. Old revival out...new revival in. As Renaissance Revival style passed out of fashion, it opened the door for the next "new" thing...a revival of the Colonial period.

But more recently, Renaissance Revival pieces have gone through another revival—a revival in value. Not too long ago a walnut baby crib with a canopy top sold at auction for over $15,000.

Oh baby!

Frankenstein Furniture

HERE'S A HORROR story that's not for the faint of heart. We call it "The Terrible Tale of the Scrambled Antiques."

When it comes to antique chairs, the more the merrier...and the more valuable. Eight chairs are better than six; ten chairs are better than twelve, and so on.

A single antique chair is the "orphan" of the industry and probably the least desirable piece of furniture there is. In fact, a pair of matched chairs is worth 50% more than two single ones.

Sometimes, however, a dealer or restoration expert will come across a small set of just 4 chairs...or possibly an odd-numbered set of 3 or 5. What to do? What to do?

The answer: cannibalism.

Not human cannibalism...furniture cannibalism. They take the chairs apart and use the pieces to make new chairs like the old ones. Sort of like Dr. Frankenstein and his monster.

How the Davenport Got Its Name

IN 1492, A certain Captain Columbus sailed the ocean blue. 300 years later in 1790, a certain Captain Davenport was doing some sailing of his own.

One thing troubled Davenport. He wanted a writing desk to take along with him, but he didn't want to take a heavy piece of furniture on-board.

A man of action, the good captain commissioned furniture makers Gillow and Barton of Lancaster, England to find a solution. And indeed they did. It was the birth of the compact writing desk.

Davenport loved his desk…and so did everyone else.

Every time the company received a new order for a similar item, it recorded the transaction under the name of the original purchaser. Thus, the name "Davenport" became associated with this type of desk.

How can you spot a Davenport? There is some variety to the desks, but most were characterized by a roughly square case and a slant-top writing surface.

What makes a Davenport extra special is the bank of drawers on one side of the pedestal base and the space under the writing section that allows you to store accessories such as letters, pens, stamps, etc.

Davenport-type desks are popular with modern collectors because their small size is in proper proportion to most modern room sizes. But while Davenports aren't too big, their price tag can be…

One in good condition can set you back around $5,000.

IT'S ABOUT TIME

~ ABOUT CLOCKS, CALENDARS AND TIMEPIECES ~

"There is never enough time, unless you're serving it."
~ Malcolm Forbes

"Time, time, time, see what's become of me…"
~ Paul Simon

TIMEPIECES AND CALENDARS are the instruments that measure existence. They can be very simple like a stick in a circle (or a primitive sundial), or extremely complex like a modern chronograph. They can go with us as we travel (on our wrist or in our pocket) or stand guard in our homes (on shelves or on the floor). They all serve the same purpose, but have an incredible variety of shapes, styles, sizes, and movements.

The first timepiece was really the sun. It came up and then went down. Came up again. We've had one day. Whether Adam realized the earth revolved around the sun or vice-versa makes no difference. The event of the passage of time was calculated in numerical fashion. One could differentiate amounts of time by days-easily done on a grid. However, people needed a more exact way to separate time during that day. In other words, "come to my house at sundown" was easily understood, but "come to my house in 1/20th of a day" was not.

You know the rest, don't you? Days became broken into hours, hours into minutes, etc. This needs standardization, however, since my hours and minutes may not be the same as your hour and minutes (beach time). That's the whole point of clocks, timepieces, and calendars. We've got to be able to meet for lunch at the same time, otherwise the food gets cold and the beer gets warm!

Fortunately, the human race has agreed on a standard of time. Somewhere in the world there exists the perfect clock. It measures minutes in an exact way (60 seconds to the minute). Everyone who makes a clock must go to this place (unknown to the rest of the world) and synchronize their products to the master. They then place a small piece of tape over the pendulum, spring, or battery that can't be touched until the purchaser removes it. Once removed, the clock will keep accurate time until the weights hit bottom, the spring is "un-sprung", or the battery runs dry. At this point of time, one must usually re-wind the instrument with a special key or run to the local drugstore to find the identical small dial of energy that will fit in the select spot. Unfortunately, the store never has the right dial, so this task becomes time consuming.

Every once in a while (usually once a year, when least expected), the clock breaks. It doesn't fall apart, but it just kind of loses its get up and go. It seems to always be late. Rarely does it maintain the same readings as all the other timepieces you own, and often needs manual correction. This becomes a real pain in the neck. It also takes valuable time. When this begins to affect our lives, like missing important traffic updates on the radio, we go ballistic.

It's either time for a new timepiece or time to find a repairman to fix the erratic one. Finding a new timepiece is easy, but finding a good repair-person (notice I didn't say man), is hell. These people are reclusive. They are cranky. They are unsociable. Perhaps it's because they sit in a room with a million clocks all ticking at the same time (if they're good repair persons).

Mind you, they don't go to school for this. It would take up too much time. Instead, they learn their trade through experience. To me, that says trial and error. They learn by breaking clocks and trying to fix them. They learn by looking at broken clocks and deeming them unfixable. Then they hide them in the back room in case another one comes in just like it. Maybe they'll find one that works and they can see what might be missing, bent, or stuck.

In any case, they work on your clock. It always takes forever. They have a sign hanging up over their desk. It says "we will fix no clock before it is time." I think that means that they fix it when their next tax bill comes in the mail. Not really, these are good chaps. The real reason it takes so long is not the parts (they're small) or labor (these are not heavy parts), but the accuracy.

All clock repair people must check the accuracy of their repairs. That means they must travel incognito to some place in the world to the master clock. They must synchronize the clocks. That's an expensive proposition. They don't just take one clock, but all the clocks they've been working on for a whole year.

This insures the world that time is right. It's also why the clock repair-person gets so much money for so little work.

Ticking off Differences

WHAT'S THE DIFFERENCE between a clock and a timepiece?

Don't get suspicious…this isn't another one of our trick questions. There really is a legitimate difference between the two.

When Brian tried to figure this one out, his first guess was that a time-piece was older. (Sorry, Brian, that's a "No.") Then he was stumped because he could only figure out what made them alike…the fact that they both tell time.

Maybe the "hint" that helped him will help you: A timepiece is known as a "T"…but a clock is known as a "T" and "S".

The "T" stands for "Time" and the "S" stands for "Strike." So the differ-ence is that a timepiece tells time, but a clock tells time AND strikes the hour…or half-hour…or quarter-hour.

A sundial is a timepiece…although you probably wouldn't want to strap one to your wrist. An hourglass is a timepiece. So's an egg timer. They are all used to measure the passage of time.

A clock is like the 2.0 version of a timepiece. As well as keeping track of

> **Ding Dong School**
> The word clock was first used in the 14th Century. It comes from "clocca," the Latin word for bell.

the hours and minutes as they go by, *this* timepiece offers the added bonus of an audible striking mechanism that gongs, rings, or chimes.

Time on the Move

HAVE YOU EVER seen a carriage clock?

No! Not a little LED display that you put in baby's stroller! A *carriage clock*...the 19th Century equivalent of a traveling alarm clock.

Carriage clocks were all the rage in the 1800's. While a few were manufactured in England, nearly all carriage clocks were made in France until the early 20th Century. Simple and functional, they were made of either brass or bronze.

The clocks stood from 4-7" high and had a small handle so that they could be carried easily. And they usually had white faces and black numerals so they could be read by moonlight. (How clever!)

Clocks with subsidiary dials were especially desirable. In addition to the hours and minutes, these clocks could also show the days of the week or sound an alarm.

(For Brian, any alarm that doesn't include a "snooze button" isn't worth having.)

> **All Dressed Up**
> Engraved-case carriage clocks are more valuable than plain ones. The *most* valuable have elaborate, detailed decorations that cover as much of the case as possible.

The most elegant carriage clocks had cloisonné or porcelain cases. Others had leather cases. Through the years, those cases have been lost and only the clocks remain.

The Granddaddy of Them All

HOW DO YOU ring in the New Year? One of the best ways we know is with a chiming grandfather clock.

When does a clock deserve to be called a grandfather?

A grandfather has a face (but not wrinkles) and a pendulum enclosed in a wooden case. The cases were usually made of walnut, mahogany, oak, maple, cherry or elm.

Like most grandfathers, these clocks were originally known by another name…a "tall case clock."

The 'big boys' stood between 6 and 9 feet tall. They had to. There needed to be enough room for the long, swinging pendulum and the weights.

So where did the term 'grandfather clock' come from? Around 1875, the song "My Grandfather's Clock" became popular, and soon the tall clocks were given a new nickname.

Some qualities that make grandfathers valuable are decorated faces, the maker's name or label somewhere on the clock, inlaid cases and an unusual top with added finials.

What does a good grandfather cost these days? A clock made before 1840 in America sells for about $5,000 to $10,000…or more.

But here's a surprise: a new grandfather can cost almost as much!

> A tall case clock that's not so tall--less than 6 feet-- has another name. It is appropriately referred to as a "grandmother" clock… after the "little woman."

Finding Lost Time

YOU'D THINK THAT yesterday's calendars—like yesterday's newspaper—wouldn't be fit for anything but getting a fire going in your fireplace.

But, in fact, calendars are *extremely* collectible and pretty valuable, too, depending on the subject matter. Value is also determined by whether or not it's an original calendar or just a reproduction.

At auctions, antique fairs, and flea markets, for example, original beer calendars are always a hot item, selling for up to $1,000 when they're in good shape.

Unfortunately, because of the way they were made (with inexpensive paper) and used (taped or tacked onto a surface), vintages calendars in good condition are few and far between. And that's a shame, too, because calendars are like little "looking glasses" into the past, featuring the products and famous faces of their time.

From Brian's Personal Collection

As early as the 1800, calendars were used as promotional items. I've got calendars from the Berlin Iron Bridge Company from 1897 and Dr. Daniel's Medicated Dog and Puppy Bread from 1913."

In the 1950's, product pictures gave way to people pictures. Although kittens, puppies, and tranquil landscapes were popular, pin-ups were the rage. In 1952, the undisputed "king" of pin-up calendars burst onto the scene. The calendar featured a nude picture of Hollywood queen Marilyn Monroe.

It was scandalous and hugely popular.

In December 1953, a not-yet-well-known ladies' man bought the rights to reproduce the "Golden Dreams" photograph. The following year, Hugh Hefner made Marilyn Monroe the first centerfold in the first ever issue of *Playboy* magazine.

Although the first *Playboy* magazines have value as collectibles, most of the later issues do not. But that hasn't stopped generations of men and boys from keeping a *Playboy* stash just for the fun of it.

PLAY WITH ME

~ ABOUT TOYS ~

The difference between men and boys
is the price of their toys

Oh, You Beautiful Doll

CAN YOU NAME this Hollywood superstar?

> She was everyone's favorite "little princess:" a charming, self-reliant "bright eyes" who rose to stardom during the Depression and was appointed as a delegate to the U.N. General Assembly by President Nixon in 1969.

> She was the most popular movie star in America and remains one of the most enduring child stars of all time. She's celebrated more than 70 "happy returns of the day" on her birthday: April 23rd.

Why, it's Shirley Temple, of course!

The Academy Award-winning youngster's box office bonanza helped save a major studio from bankruptcy. And the collectibles that feature her image are keeping auctions, flea markets, and antiques shops "in the chips," too.

Leon says, "There have been lots of Shirley Temple memorabilia through the years. Brian is old enough to remember a dyed-in-the-wool original: cobalt blue cereal bowls with the adorable face of "curly top" given away as premiums by Bisquick and Wheaties."

For most folks over a certain age, however, the ultimate gotta-have-it collectible was…and still is…a wide-eyed doll with cascades of Shirley's signature sausage curls.

The first Shirley Temple doll was "born" to the Ideal Toy Company in 1934. A 20" composition doll with original dress, wig, and box could bring up to $1,000.

If you've got one tucked away in *your* attic, congratulations! Your ship has come in!

It's the *Good Ship Lollipop!*

R2-D2

THIS LITTLE TIDBIT is perfect to toss out at cocktail parties, especially when people are talking movie trivia.

`In 1973, *American Graffiti* hit theaters and became an instant blockbuster. It made Richard Dreyfuss and Harrison Ford big stars and earned director George Lucas a carload of money.

But *American Graffiti* provided more than a glimpse at life in the 1950's; it was the "inspiration" for a future Lucas blockbuster… "*Star Wars.*"

Sure, Harrison Ford would "grow up" to become Hans Solo, but there's another iconic Star Wars character that was discovered…

Or perhaps we should say "*who* was discovered."

Here's the back-lot "back story":

Soundtracks are logged by reel and dialogue numbers. During the editing of *American Graffiti*, George Lucas asked the audio guys for a particular piece of the soundtrack—Reel Two, Dialogue Two.

No one remembers what was on the track, but they do remember the "shorthand" he used when he wrote down his request: R2—for Reel Two and D2 for Dialogue Two.

And that's how the 'droid that helped save the empire got his named—R2-D2.

(Or so the story goes).

R2-D2 may have helped save the space collectibles empire, as well. Some of the original Star Wars figures sell for thousands of dollars.

America's Sweetheart

WHEN RUTH AND Elliot Handler took their "little girl" to her first "coming out party," they had no way of knowing that she'd instantly become the toast of the town…a sought-after object of desire…and the centerpiece of a billion dollar empire.

Her name: Barbie!

The Handlers were the founders of Mattel Toys and named the new doll after their real life daughter Barbara. They unveiled their curvaceous creation in 1959 at the American Toy Fair in New York City.

A German doll named Lili was the inspiration for Barbie. Lili, in turn, had been modeled after a character in a racy European cartoon strip. And unlike her wholesome American cousin, Lili was marketed as a novelty item for adults, not little girls.

When Mattel bought the rights to Lili, they "cleaned up" her image and transformed the lusty Teutonic tootsie into an all-American girl…blonde-haired and blue-eyed.

The first Barbie was dolled-up in a black and white striped one-piece bathing suit and retailed for just $3. Today, that same Barbie (in an undamaged original box) can sell for $5,000!

During the first year of her introduction, 351,000 Barbie dolls were sold, and despite her age, she's as popular as ever:

> Mattel claims that in every second of every day,
> two Barbie dolls are sold somewhere in the world!

Barbie, you're just like vintage wine. The older you get, the more we love you. And we hope you're around forever!

Playing With Dolls

IN THE 1950'S, when we'd go out for a spin in the family sedan, it was fun to look for bobbleheads…the wiggly, jiggly figures that people put on their dashboard or in their rear window.

Usually you'd spot animals and human figures with their heads in motion, but the popular ukulele-playing hula girl had hips that bobbled with every bump. We thought they were the latest, greatest things on earth.

We were wrong…by a hundred years.

Bobbleheads were always on the winning team when it comes to sports.

A New York Knick was one of the first bobbleheads offered back in the 1920's. But it wasn't until forty years later that the bobblehead phenomenon scored a homer…thanks to baseball.

> Bobbleheads are a "sub-set" of a novelty group known as nodders and swayers. They were first produced in Germany and later in Japan from the German molds in the latter half of the 19th Century…

A series of bobbleheads was created for each team to sell at stadiums all over the country. The dolls were of papier-mâché and featured a small boy's face wearing a baseball cap.

But the "face" of the bobblehead industry was about to change: to cash in on the great 4-day home-run race of 1961, bobbleheads were created with the faces of baseball's greatest sluggers—Mickey Mantle, Roger Maris, Willie Mays and Roberto Clemente.

It was the re-birth of celebrity bobbleheads.

You'll Shoot Your Eye Out

(This one's for Ralphie!)

YOU'D PROBABLY NEVER guess, but the first BB gun was actually made by a company that made farmers' windmills. The Plymouth Iron Windmill Company of Plymouth, Michigan originated in the 1880's. They harnessed wind power to pump water to much of the Midwest.

As the need for windmills diminished, and the future of electricity became clearer, the company sought a product to keep the firm alive. In

1886 a metal and wire contraption was invented that shot a lead ball using compressed air. This gun like apparatus was exhibited to the president of the company, who reportedly said, "you could shoot your eye out." NO he didn't. He said, "Boy, that's a daisy."

The name stuck—both to the gun and the company. By 1895 the company made more Daisy BB guns than windmills and changed its name to Daisy Manufacturing Company.

These "air rifles" continued to be popular for many years, including during the Depression. Daisy joined with comic strip creators to make other premiums (giveaways) and toys. In 1929 they created several space age guns for the Buck Rogers' character. One of them was the Buck Rogers' Atomic Detonator Pistol. These are the forerunners of all the space age robots, ray guns, and even Star Wars memorabilia. (Every kid should have one.)

The company then turned to another comic strip, Bronc Peeler. Never heard of him? Well, maybe not, but maybe you can remember a minor character from the strip called Red. Red Ryder.

Daisy named a new rifle after him, The Red Ryder special. It became a household name (just ask Ralphie). More than nine million Red Ryders were sold (and we're still counting).

The Red Ryder has become a symbol of much of older America and Christmas. Who knows which has become more popular, the gun or the lace stocking leg lamp? It seems the Red Ryder has been around for a heck of a lot longer. I'd stake the ranch on it.

The only problem is—you might shoot your eye out!

TIP: According to Tim Like, author of *Toys From American Childhood*, all Daisy products have the name of the company, DAISY MFG and patent information somewhere on the gun. It's not inside the barrel, however.

Quackers

CICKITTY CLACK...CLICKITTY Clack. Pull the string. Hear it quack.

Question: What's made of wood with a paper label and makes a noise when pulled by a string?

The answer: either a Katy Kackler or Snap-Quack Duck-both made by the same company.

We're sure you remember these toys. They've been popular for more than sixty years, first in wood and then plastic. The Fisher-Price Toy Company started in 1930 in New York State. They quickly gained attention when their very first shipment was delivered to Macy's in New York City. By the end of the following year nearly seven hundred stores carried the new Fisher-Price line (a group of sixteen colorful figures or animals).

Fisher-Price became known for their whimsical, friendly toys that mimicked farm animals or nature. Luckily the timeframe saw the creation of the Disney characters and Fisher-Price added Mickey, Popeye, and Donald to their lines.

The FP toys were based on the mission of the firm. They sought toys that were ingenious, had "intrinsic play value" (whatever that is), were made well, included some sort of action (walking, rolling, or clucking), and were good value for the price.

The company was particularly proud of their well-executed paper labels. They were colorful, bold, and carried a lot of detail. Although the paper often ripped or chipped, for the most part they stood up well.

Collectors often date the pieces according to the construction. If the piece is all wood it was probably produced before 1949. If it is completely plastic it is probably after 1964. Any combination dates it in the middle.

All FP toys are marked (Halleluiah)! The company logo is usually in black and carries the product number of the toy. For example, #141 Snap-Quack is an all-wood Mallard duck with paper label that has red wheels. (The duck was designed by famous wildlife artist Lynn Bogue.)

Even the plastic ones have some value, although only a small fraction of the wood.

We used to make fun of Jumbo the Xylophone player, Pushy the Elephant, and Uncle Timmy Turtle. No more.

What's made of wood with a paper label and makes a noise when pulled by a string?

An investment.

The Original Wooden Lego

WE KNOW THAT *Lego* began in 1934 in Denmark. Not to take anything away from Ole Kirk Christainsen, but the idea of putting things together has been around a long time, however. It hit another guy, Charles Pajeau, in Evanston, Illinois a few decades earlier.

Charles, a tombstone cutter (not exactly a flashy job), got an idea for toys while watching his kids play with wooden spools and knitting needles. No, it wasn't blocks or pick-up sticks, but it was a version of both.

He borrowed the design of the wooden spool with holes, and the round needles to develop a construction technique that has thrilled kids for many years. After "tinkering" with it for a while, he set up a prototype and sought to sell it to the world. At the New York Toy Fair in 1915 he was assigned a spot in a far corner. He didn't sell one unit!

On his way home, Charles convinced two drugstores in Grand Central Terminal to carry his toy, in exchange for a hefty commission. Next came window displays that involved complex creations made of these spools and rods. He even placed fans nearby to move framework windmills with bladed tops.

Just like *Lego*, part of the selling technique was the finished product and the creative energy of the makers. Pajeau hired men to sit in windows building structures from his units. Kids began to get the idea. Since that day in New York City, over 200 million sets of *Tinkertoys* have been sold!

As with *Lego*, part of the desire of these sets is the enjoyment of creation and construction. Since they are mass-produced from identical parts, the collecting of either product line is not the same as finished products like toy trucks, dolls, or board games. But time will tell and complete sets of either *Tinkertoys* or *Legos*, or any other construction type toy will remain popular.

The key to their present value is the presence of the original packaging, the complete set with any instructional booklet, and the condition of the pieces. Although Charles Pajeau doesn't have a Tinkertoy Land named after him, he does have a spot in the heart of all kid contractors-and even adults.

Sometimes just tinkering around is a lot of fun!

PS: We're glad Charles didn't event a tombstone cutter game. Could have called it the "cut of death." Wouldn't have been the same.

DISHING IT UP

~ ABOUT POTTERY, PORCELAIN, AND CERAMICS ~

Historical relics—jugs, vases, storage and carrying vessels—
are often cited as examples of human advancement,
evolution and sophistication.

And you thought it was just a cereal bowl!

THIS IS A SHORT chapter on china—not the country, the object. It seems that human exploration, deception, and even wars have been fought over the discovery of a certain formula...one that delineates the ingredients of a hard, ceramic substance called porcelain.

Porcelain, you see, is a very fine, translucent object that is non-porous and can be used to hold both hot and cold food, liquids, or objects. Decorative pieces with nice, shiny surfaces are often used for formal dining and showing off one's wealth.

When compared to fine porcelain, pottery is a very heavy, dark, and porous ceramic that can be decorated, but not as easily. It is rather clumsy, compared to porcelain, and often is seen as a stepchild. It was made for common purposes, such as holding whiskey, salt, or flour.

America has always had a good deal of pottery. It's made from common clay and can be formed by either itinerants or local potters. It's not very pretty, however, and was never seen as something glamorous.

Porcelain, on the other hand, was always considered elegant. Even in the 17th and 18th centuries, it was desired for use and trade. Even Marco Polo reportedly admitted that his real quest in the Orient was finding the holy grail of ceramics: porcelain. As were others, since we began trading heavily with England and others who were buying blue and white porcelains from China.

That type of porcelain was called "Chinese export porcelain," and it was made for us hungry westerners. It had all the right stuff. It was fine. It was translucent. It was decorated in wonderful patterns and scenes. It didn't absorb liquid (great for eating)...but it was EXPENSIVE.

The reason it was expensive is that the Chinese knew the secret ingredient...and we didn't. It was called kaolin (a special clay or soil). The entire rest of the world longed for the secret and fought many battles, real and scientific, for the treasure. Finally, a few Westerners succeeded. In Germany, it was the people in Meissen; in France, the district of Sevres, and in England, a little belatedly, it was Wedgwood. America...sorry, you never got it. It wasn't until the late 1800's that we finally produced a decent product (the forerunners of Lenox). By then it was too late. We were stuck with pottery. (But stuck in a very good way, since we excelled in it and began to make some of the best pottery ever seen.)

So you see, the story IS about China—the country and not the object. For nothing really exists called china. It's either pottery or porcelain or somewhere in between. It's not china!

A Royal Treatment for Santa

WHEN YOU THINK about a "Christmas plate," you probably envision a dish of holiday sugar cookies piled high by your kids as a "thank you" to Santa for his visit.

Well, if Santa's anything like Leon, he's more interested in the value of the plate than in the flavor of the cookies!

Christmas plates are collectibles. Many companies come out with a new plate each year, in a tradition that started in the late 19th Century. In 1895, a company called Bing and Groendahl offered *Behind the Frozen Window,* and it sold for 60-cents.

A new century brought a new 'contender' for the hearts of Christmas shoppers. And in 1908, the Royal Copenhagen company got into the spirit of the season with their *Madonna with Child* plate. Both were immediate "must haves."

So how did those decorative plates end up as cookie carriers?

Blame it on the Danish!

B&G and Royal Copenhagen were both based in Denmark. The tradition in that country is to give the hired help plates of homemade goodies at Christmas time—cake-like aebleskivers, spicy sebernodder, and sweet, buttery spritz cookies.

(You could gain weight just *thinking* about 'em!)

You can't put a price on homemade, but you can put a price on vintage Christmas plates. The first Royal Copenhagen plate lists at $5,000 and the first B&G plate can run anywhere from $6,000-$8,000.

Ho, ho, holy cow! You can buy a lot of cookies with that money.

> ### Affordable History
> In 1915, to honor twenty years of Christmas plates, B&G issued their first Jubilee plate--a reproduction of *Behind the Froze Window*-- and have continued to issue a Jubilee plate every five years. Values for vintage plates range from $18 to $150. More recent plates, though collectible, are worth less...at least for now!

If Two Heads Are Better Than One, How About Three Names...

WHAT STARTED AS a little "Hill" turned into a mountain of Fulper... Stangl...and Pfaltzgraf.

In 1805, Samuel Hill opened Hill Pottery. Hill was a utilitarian potter, rather than an artist, producing drain pipes, storage crocks, and jars. And he used what was at hand—the red clay of Flemington, New Jersey.

Enter Abraham Fulper.

Hill died in 1858 and pottery worker Abram Fulper stepped in. By the 1860's, the re-named Fulper Pottery was producing an assortment of earthenware, stoneware, and tile products. The most notable was Fulper's patented Germ-Proof Filter, a forerunner of today's "water cooler."

But wait! There's more.

In 1910, William Fulper hired ceramic engineer Martin Stangl to develop new glazes and shapes for him. One of Stangl's first design projects was the unusual Vasekraft line, pottery lamps that were topped by pottery shades inset with stained glass shapes and panels.

Stangl's Vasekraft lamps were expensive even then…and more so today. One of the company's cockatoo perfume lamps recently sold on eBay for $695!

But wait…there's *still* more.

In 1930, Stangl bought the place and re-named it again. You guessed it: Stangl Pottery!

Stangl's colorful, simple designs made the company's dinnerware a casual alternative to more formal styles. At the same time, its art pottery lines competed successfully with more expensive and sophisticated ware.

From the 1930's through 1978, there were often as many as 1000 patrons visiting Stangl's Flemington showrooms each year. Automobile clubs and tour bus lines often included the Stangl Outlet as an integral part of many road trips.

And Pfaltzgraff? The Pfaltzgraff company purchased the Stangl Pottery facilities in 1978.

But stay tuned. Who knows when there will be more to tell!

Rook My World

ROOKWOOD POTTERY IS one of the hottest collectibles in today's market. It's possibly the most famous after the super-popular Roseville. The pieces blend in well with Mission Oak and can be either a dull matte or high-glazed finish.

Like a lot of potteries, Rookwood started in Ohio around 1880.

At that time, it was common for wealthy women to paint blank ceramics as a pastime. Rookwood founder Maria Nichols Storer enjoyed the pastime but decided she needed to turn up the heat.

Storer was especially interested in different glazes. As she experimented, she became frustrated with the firing temperatures provided by the local kiln. Dissatisfied with the limited results he was able to achieve, Storer decided to buy her own kiln.

Rookwood Pottery was born. The factory continued to produce until 1960, but most of the best pieces were made up to the 1920's.

> How did Rookwood get its name? The company was named for Marie Storer's family home, which was also home to a large number of crows. But rather than crowswood, or ravenswood, she called it Rookswood...a synonym for crows.

Rookwood pieces were designed, made, and hand-painted by the artist. They are a favorite among collectors because they are beautiful and well-marked, too. The base carries factory marks, including a symbol for or the name, Rookwood, as well as a dating system

Rookwood is beautiful, well-marked, collectible, and also frequently imitated.

So how can you protect yourself against getting "rooked" when looking at Rookwood? Most pieces are marked with a flame design over a reversed R and letter P.

Looking East

ORIENTAL ART, CERAMICS, and collectibles come together in perfect harmony in an Asian collectible called "Satsuma." It takes its name from a warlord who brought Korean potters to Japan in the early 1600's.

Satsuma is a faience..."antique talk" for tin-glazed pottery. It's known for rainbow bright enamels in blue, red, green, orange, and gold, as well as exquisite miniature paintings.

Prior to 1900, finer pieces adhered to the old cream-colored body covered with a

American Satsuma
Most of the Satsuma in today's market is from the 20th century...and not quite as valuable. During the First World War, Americans were unable to buy undecorated porcelains from Europe. But with "Yankee Ingenuity," they decided to decorate plain Satsuma ware that was still being imported.

This East-meets-West marriage resulted in the term "American Satsuma."

finely crackled glaze. This is a hallmark of Satsuma and gives the illusion that the glaze is cracked.

Satsuma ware from the late 19th and early 20th Century is the most coveted. A 25" Satsuma dragon vase from 1911 is reportedly worth $6900.

Dresden in Meissen

ASK A GERMAN the difference between "Dresden" and "Meissen" and they'll tell you "About 15 miles."

Ask us the same question, and we'll say, "No difference." That's because *we're* talking about porcelain...porcelain in Germany.

Elector Frederick Augustus I—King August the Strong to his friends—planned to make his home in Dresden the most important royal residence in the world. He set out to discover the secret to creating Chinese "white gold"—hard paste porcelain.

One Dark Night

Much of the work and the history of all the porcelain produced in Dresden and Meissen was destroyed in a massive Allied bombing raid during World War II. In a single night, most Dresden decorating studios were demolished along with many historical documents. The porcelain painting business never fully recovered.

In 1710, the King's first factory—the Royal Saxon Porcelain Manufactory—was built fifteen miles from Dresden in the city of Meissen. But since Dresden was the cultural and economic center of Saxony, most Meissen porcelain was sold "out of town" in Dresden.

In a very short time, buyers began to incorrectly refer to their purchases as "Dresden china." Dresden dinnerware was all the rage, but it was the Dresden lace figurines that were truly coveted.

"Dresden lace," was a process in which real lace was dipped in liquid porcelain and then applied to the figures by hand. The result was a stunningly delicate appearance that was almost indistinguishable from soft fabric.

NO STONE-THROWING ZONE

~ ABOUT COLLECTIBLE GLASS ~

People in glass houses
should change clothes in the basement

GLASS IS A VERY strange object. For example, furniture is made of wood. Paper is made of trees or fiber. A textile is made of cloth-usually cotton, wool, or silk. But glass, glass is made of sand. That makes no sense.

How can one object be made out of a completely foreign and dissimilar compound? One is grainy, dirty, dark, and sticks to your wet feet, and the other is smooth, clean, light, and water slides right off it. The answer is fire!

Right. Fire. You got it.

Heat the sand up and it turns to glass. Make sure you add silica or it just won't work. It doesn't really become glass (like a beer bottle), but it does become a molten mess. This globular mess is usually blown by someone with a long pipe (a pontil) or placed into a mold and then cooled. The result in either case is a piece of glass.

Although for many, many years the only way to make glass was to blow it through a tube (like making soap bubbles), an early Victorian inventor created molds that made the job a lot easier and much more productive.

The fact that glass is made from sand and silica makes it relatively cheap. (Have you ever paid a lot of money for a bag of sand?) So how come glass can be so expensive?

The answer is not the glass itself, but what someone does with the glass. You can change formulas and add chemicals or elements to the basic formula (Tiffany's favrille glass), you can make elaborate patterns in molds (pattern glass), you can artistically design the surface by grinding it (cut or engraved glass), you can paint the surface (Victorian painted glass), you can add colors to the molten mess (Victorian Art Glass), or you can experiment in any number of combinations.

The key to antique glass is the rarity of the design, particularly if it is made from a mold, or the amount of handwork in the finished product. One that is pushed out of a mold and then sold is a lot less valuable than one that is made as a blank, cut on a copper wheel by a craftsman, then polished and gilt by a finisher. Age has very little to do with it. (Not nothing to do with it, just very little.)

People tend to collect pattern glass because it's easier to find and identify. One would rather have a collection of 20 pieces than just one. You also don't have to know a lot about the product—just the patterns, shapes, and colors, the information of which is available in many books.

One of a kind glass is a lot harder, both to identify and to value. But there are lots of references, museums, auctions, and collectors for help. Beware! Collecting glass can be habit forming. (Ever heard of a person having a collection of one piece of depression or carnival glass?)

Oh, by the way. Glass also breaks. It's made out of sand, heated by fire, and breaks. Who would have thought?

Does That Glass Come With Chips?

THINK YOU KNOW your decorative glass? *We'll* be the judges of that!

The following multiple-choice question will put you to the test:

What is SANDWICH GLASS?
a) a bread plate
b) glass with 3 layers
c) glass cut into the shape of ham and cheese on rye
d) none of the above

The correct answer is, of course, "d."

The name "Sandwich Glass" isn't some coy or cutesy reference to the shape or composition of the glass. Sandwich glass is simply glass produced in Sandwich, Massachusetts in the mid- to late-1800's, most notably at the Boston & Sandwich Glass Company. Deming Jarves, the man known as the creator of pressed glass, founded the Sandwich Glass company.

Boston & Sandwich Glass cracked in 1890 and went out of business. But there was still a lot of interest in the lacy, pressed glass that used the blown molded technique.

Enter "commerce."

In another example of "imitation is the sincerest form of flattery"…and a brilliant way to make money…"sandwich glass" became a term used for specific patterns inspired by the original Sandwich glassmakers but created by non-Sandwich companies.

Sandwich Kings

There are four major makers of Sandwich pattern glass: Anchor Hocking, Duncan & Miller, Indiana Glass, and Westmoreland Glass.

The phrase "Sandwich pattern" would be more in the spirit of "truth in advertising."

Glasses to Flip Over

"GLASS TUMBLERS"…SOUNDS like the featured act in the latest Cirque du Soleil presentation, doesn't it?

Glass tumblers are actually water glasses. But don't sell them short. They are more than just an alternative to drinking your Perrier straight from the bottle!

Glass tumblers are beautiful forms of colored Victorian decorative glass. They're 'art' that you can sip from.

These classy glasses were manufactured by different companies to match other items in their production line…mostly water and lemonade pitchers.

But why are they called tumblers?

Originally, you held tumblers in your in your hand until your drink was finished…or else.

Primary Colors

The 'art' of glass tumblers extended to the colors used to make them. Instead of just red and yellow, you'll find glass tumblers in colors like rubina, peachblow, and amberina.

(Color me educated!)

Or else what?

Or else you could say good-bye to the contents! Tumblers had rounded bottoms, so you couldn't set them down without spilling your drink.

So these tumblers were also clowns! But their prices are nothing to laugh about. Some vintage glass tumblers sell for as much as $500!

Hey…maybe they should be under the Big Top. "Ladies and gentlemen, and children of all ages…in the center ring…please put your hands together for glass tumblers!"

Pressing Matters

WE'VE GOT ANOTHER stumper for you:

What's at home on the beach…but can be "pressed" into service at a fancy dinner table?

Glass!

Shocking…but true. Glass is actually made of liquid sand. And since the 1830's, molds have been used to make pressed and pattern glass into vases, pitchers, and bowls.

The sand mixture was heated and then poured into two- or three-part, hinged molds resembling objects we all use everyday like goblets, candy dishes, and cream 'n' sugar sets.

The process made glass available to every house in America. And the glass was crafted into every imaginable shape, size, and color.

It was transformed into relish dishes, spoons, and teapots.

Difference Between Cut and Press Glass

Seams: Pressed glass has seams left by the mold, cut glass does not.

Feel: Cut glass has a feel of elegance, and may be a thicker and heavier than pressed glass.

Ring: The lead content of cut glass produces a sustained ring when gently flicked with a finger. Pressed glass produced a "thud."

Brilliance: Cut glass reflects and refracts light. It produces a brilliance not found in pressed glass.

Smell: (just kidding)

Clean-Cut

HAVE YOU EVER seen a knife rest? (How about a barn dance?)

In the Victorian Era, the "washing machines" were people. So even if you had servants, the last thing you wanted was to have your dinner guests stain your fancy linen banquet cloths with their dirty silverware.

And in the late 19th Century, the possibilities for staining were endless. There was so much flatware on Victorian tables that it's amazing they didn't collapse under the weight!

In 1880, Reed & Barton offered a flatware line of 57 distinct pieces, including asparagus forks, bon bon spoons and tongs, lettuce forks, fish slicers, butter picks, berry and bacon forks, cheese scoops, cucumber servers and spoons for salt, bouillon, cream soup, grapefruit and orange. (Those folks knew how to eat!)

Exquisite cut-glass knife rests were extremely popular, but you can also find your own little "slice of heaven" created in silver, silver plate, horn and combinations. Individual knife rests were about 5" long and usually shaped like barbells, with large crystal balls at the end of a center rod.

Knife plates began to vanish after World War II.

Newer and less vulnerable fabrics were being created and used as table linen. That, plus advancements in washing machines and detergents, changed knife rests from a "cutting-edge" table essential to a quaint reminder of kinder, gentler time.

Okay, let's give this subject a rest!

Diamond in the Smooth

QUESTION: WHAT'S ROUND on both sides and "hi" in the middle with beautiful pressed glass all around?

Answer: Ohio. It's the birthplace of the glass with the welcoming name, Heisey (pronounced "Hi, Zee") Glass.

A.H. Heisy was born in Germany, and lived in Pennsylvania, but he got "on the map" in Newark, Ohio where he built his first factory.

Why is everyone so "high" on Heisey?

The A. H. Heisey company produced "elegant glassware for practical usage" from 1896 to 1957 in Newark, Ohio. The glass they created was not cheap when it was made, and it showed up in many a bride's registry during the company's "reign" from 1896-1957.

They began producing press-molded glass from older Early American pattern glass molds and moved on to make the beautiful, delicate glass that people often incorrectly refer to as "crystal."

So how do you spot a Heisy? Look for it's "brand." It's a diamond-shape around a large letter H.

The factory produced its first line of glassware in April of 1896, but the famous trademark didn't appeal until 1900. The idea for the design came from the fraternity pin of Heisey's son.

The mark is sometimes extremely well hidden and you'll need to check a glass from stem to stern to find it…although it's likely to be on the stem.

Why? The trademark was pressed into the glass, so it had to appear on the press-molded portion of the glass…usually the stem.

Girls Love Carboys…and So Do Winemakers

CARBOYS ARE NOT chauffeurs…and they will never be pressed into service 'driving' Miss Daisy. But they will provide her with a lovely glass of her favorite 'red' or 'black.'

In the world of winemaking, a carboy is a glass or plastic container that looks like a large jug…kind of like the bottle on the office water-cooler. They're used for fermenting juice, carrying out secondary fermentations, and for storing wine on a long term basis.

As well as being used by winemakers, vintage carboys were "pressed into service" as containers for molasses, olive oil, and other liquids. They are especially collectible because each mouth-blown and hand-finished piece is unique.

No two are exactly the same.

The shapes are unbelievable. You can find ovoid, kidney, cylindrical, round, teardrop, apple, and heart-shaped carboys. The colors are extraordinary, too. There's olive green and aqua, and also pieces in amber and the ultra-rare cobalt blue.

Carboys are a perfect example of "industrial art" with historical and aesthetic appeal.

Now *demijohns* are the "little fellas" of the bottle business. They have the same shape and function as a carboy, although they are significantly smaller. But although they may be smaller in stature, they're still big in appeal.

So drink up!

> **Wrapping Things Up**
> Carboys and demijohns were often "dressed up" in elaborately woven wicker or raffia at the glass factory. As well as looking good, the "wraps" helped ensure that the bottles made it to their respective destinations in one piece!

Even Bottles Have to Watch Their Figurals

EVERYONE SEEMS TO have a "thing" for figural bottles. How about you?

What? You're not familiar with figurals?

Figurals are objects—everything from jewelry to napkin rings, spoon holders, and bottles—that are shaped like something else, most often a person or an animal.

Just think of Mrs. Butterworth and her bottled pancake syrup!

One of the earliest known figural "bottles" is a multicolored fish from Egypt. It dates back to 1352-1336 B.C. and was probably used to hold scented oil.

Despite their ancient history, figurals are alive and well. And the figural bottles that people seem to love best are liquor bottles…especially whiskey bottles. One of the most famous figurals is the amber E.G. Booz Old Cabin Whiskey bottle. It was made in the shape of…

An old cabin, of course!

From 1964-1985, the Ezra Brooks company produced more than 300 different Kentucky whiskey figural bottles, such as American Legion commemoratives, and exotic animals, fancy cars.

Most figurals are listed for under $50. While they're not especially valuable, they *are* very collectible.

> **Half Empty or Half Full**
> Opening up your figural liquor bottle to take a swig is gonna cost you. The bottle is worth more if both it, and the liquor inside, are intact. In other words: "bottoms up" means "prices down."

You might want to refer to your liquor cabinet as your "figural glass collection"...Brian does. But that's stretching it a bit.

What better way to drink than from a stein? A stein is a mug specially made for beer or ale. Usually it is made of stoneware, porcelain, or pottery and has a hinged lid to keep it from spilling as one wanders around the room. They range in size from 1/2 a liter up to 5 liters (a krug). The Germans excelled in beer and stein making. Although the most familiar is the ceramic type with shiny tops and brightly colored molded figures of huntsmen or party goers, the best are those made by the Villeroy & Boch Company. They are called "Mettlach" and usually have a mark of a castle on the base. They often go for over $1,000. We'll drink to that as well!

Drip Dry

THERE'S NOTHING WORSE that a perfectly good wooden bar or table with "unsightly rings" left by a wet glass. And in the 1890's, you couldn't just "Pledge" your furniture back to a high gloss.

So necessity was the mother of the first "coaster"—a wood pulp cut-out that was used to keep beverages from ruining wood.

The English call them beermats. The Germans say Bierdeckel. The barkeeps called them "miracle workers. Whatever they are called, bartender and waitresses gave them away to their glass-raising patrons.

Guinness of Ireland probably holds the world record for variety. They made thousands of different beermats in every size, shape, and pattern imaginable.

Beermats became almost as popular as the beer they soaked up. Before long, bartenders were noticing that they were disappearing out of the bar...

Where did they go? Into the pockets of patrons who took them home and started hoarding them...leading to tegestology.

A disease?

No! The "art" of collecting beer coasters.

We'll drink to that!

Spike-ing Interest

YOU CAN'T WALK down the street in Toon Town without tripping over a cartoon bulldog with a spiked collar. (Think of the big, scary, pooch on steroids that's always after Bugs or Daffy).

Or step into the University of Georgia's football team locker room. Whaddya see? Bulldogs. Dozens of 'em. All with spiked collars.

What's up with that?

Are rich kids born with silver spoons in their mouths and bulldog pups born with spiked collars around their necks? Were spiked collars invented to make bulldogs (and football players) look meaner???

Museum Pieces

An extraordinary collection of 500 years' worth of antique dog collars can be found at Leeds Castle, near Maidstone, Kent. The collection traces the history of canine neckwear. Each year, more than 500,000 visitors...human...come to see 100 collars and related exhibits from medieval to Victorian times.

Art...or should we say "arf"?

Nope. Spiked collars aren't about *fashion*...they're about *function.*

Spiked collars were "in vogue" in the 19th century. They functioned as "armor" for prized hunting dogs.

British hunters outfitted their pack with the impenetrable collars as protection against the tusks and bites of the wild boar they were chasing.

But if you think the dogs were prized, wait until you hear what the dog collars are worth! One collar made in the 1820's was recently priced at $2,000.00.

Looks like the antiques market is going to the dogs...or at least their collars.

Take A Seat!

EVER HEAR THE expression bigger is better? Well, not when you're talkin' antiques it ain't.

Good things come in small packages. Sometimes these small things are worth ten times the things in big packages.

Salesman Samples are items that actually look just like the larger counterparts and work. They are not for children. Salesmen would carry these items to store or shopkeepers and show them what was available. The items were usually just as detailed as the originals. Some had fitted cases. These are usually the most valuable. Even farmers got in the act. Salesmen would bring tiny examples of windmills and threshing machines for them to examine. Look for detailed workmanship, original identification tags, and wooden cases. The difference between a Salesman Sample and a "toy" made for children is significant.

Take barber chairs…

Collectors routinely pay from $1,000 to $3,000 to snag authentic, vintage chairs, all decked out in leather, chrome and enamel.

But it turns out the "hot" seat isn't a full-sized barber's chair…it's a miniature version! A salesman's vintage "sample size" Kokek brand barber chair sold at auction for over $23,000.00.

That's more than 10 times the price of the full-sized, sit-down 'shave and a haircut, 2 bits' chair.

Doll-sized versions of stoves, tents, beds, and even coffins are also popular, proving the old antiquing adage.

Leon's Warning Flare: "Don't get burned. Beware of little cast iron stoves sold as salesman samples. Most of what you find on the market today are modern reproductions."

In A Pickle

AT A FORMAL meal, when everyone's wearing their finery, why shouldn't the pickles be decked out, too?

Pickle casters are metal-framed glass jars that hold pickles. They were popular table accessories after the Civil War until about the 1890's. It's a wonderful way to make the munchable crunchables look even more delicious.

Contemporary reproductions sell for around $75.

But for just a few dollars more, you can "go authentic" with simple vintage casters. Dating back to the late 19th Century and embellished with inexpensive metal, they sell for anywhere from $150 to about $200.

Now the finest Victorian casters were put in "fancy dress". Instead of cheap substitutes, the glass was adorned with intricately tooled silver.

An upscale pickle caster can bring in around $750.00 at auction. In fact, in Virginia in 2004, two heavily ornate pickle casters sold for $1,760.00 each.

But plain or fancy, a pickle casters glass jar must have a metal frame, lid, and tongs to be considered "properly attired." (Pickles not required.)

The New Trend Is Old Fashions

BRIAN SAYS, "VINTAGE clothing—whether it's my skinny ties or Leon's too-cool-for-school bell bottoms went out of fashion long ago. "But surprise! Everything old is new again. They're right back in style today. And that makes us hipper today than we were back in the 70's."

What makes a piece of clothing 'vintage?'

Most stores that sell vintage clothes have items from the 1940's through the 70's. But purists say that items over 100 years old qualify as "antique" rather than vintage.

They're talking about Victorian white ware, christening gowns, and even...dare we mention them...'unmentionables' (ladies' lingerie).

The Victorian era was one of abundance and excess. After the invention of electroplating, objects were made to fit every dining experience. These items were fashioned in nickel, copper, or white metal, and then silverplated in a vat or tub. The silver stuck to the surface creating a lovely table accessory that exhibited taste, wealth, and use. Consider other exotic forms created during that period, like the figural napkin ring, a caster or cruet set in a frame, the standing iced water or lemonade pitcher on a swing-handled frame with tray and goblet, the knife rest, the toast server, and all the various epergnes—just to name a few. Even though these items have no intrinsic silver value, since they have such a thin coating, they have many happy collectors.

We're not purists...or puritans either, as you can tell from the lingerie reference!

So our definition of vintage is a little broader. We think that unlike wine, vintage doesn't refer to the year a garment was made. We use 'vintage' to talk about anything of mysterious origin or unknown age.

Actually...most people use the word 'vintage' to describe an item that used to be out-of-style and worthless, but is now back in fashion...and worth plenty.

Now That's An Old Coat

Sometimes vintage clothing is much more than vintage. For example, take Gen George Armstrong Custer's coat he wore at the Battle of Little Big Horn. It was supposedly worn when he was killed on June 25, 1876. (It still has a bullet hole on the left side.) In 2002, it was sold at public auction and brought a whopping $104,655. Just imagine what Lincoln's suit coat might bring? (Was he wearing a suit coat?) Guess I'll have to ask Brian.

So hang on to those too wide ties, too narrow pants, and too pointy shoes. Don't discard anything just because it's 'too-too.' One day, instead of hiding a trunk full of fashion faux pas...

You'll be advertising a treasure chest of "vintage clothing" on eBay.

HOLLYWOOD: TALES FROM TINSELTOWN

~ ABOUT HOLLYWOOD AND THE MOVIES ~

"Hollywood is where they shoot too many pictures
and not enough actors."
~ Walter Winchell

SO WHAT IS the first great Hollywood movie or movie character people started collecting? Was it Charlie Chaplin, Marilyn Monroe, or *Star Wars*? Bet the answer might surprise you.

We don't think it was any of the above. In fact, we think it probably human, and it also wasn't *Star Wars*—although that 1977 movie was probably the first to actually market the characters in a big way and create a whole new collectible.

The answer is most probably Mickey Mouse. Disney combined the magic of the animal kingdom with the big screen and created memorable characters that were sought by children and adults alike. The 1932 *Klondike Kid* movie poster sold at auction in 1995 for $57,000. Disney created generations of children who adored their loveable family. Movies spawned books, toys, dolls, trinkets, and decorations. That made Walt almost as famous as his mice.

As the movie industry grew, so did its history (makes sense). As in anything else, once you have history you have historians—people who want to keep a record of that history. In the movies, we have some people within the industry keeping the memories alive and fueling the price and demand of older material—whether it be the films themselves, the theater posters and advertisements, or the "kitcsch" (a nice word for junk) that went along with it.

Take some examples: Director Martin Scorsese collects posters. He hangs them in his New York offices. (If he gets enough, they may finally give him an Academy Award for the collection.) Leonardo Di Caprio collects mementos from *Star Wars* and horror films. (Don't know if he collects *Titanic* memorabilia-but he should have.) Michael Jackson collects all kind of Hollywood kitcsch-favoring...(this is really true) the Three Stooges and posters of child actors.

Our point is not the absurdity of the collector, but the vastness of the possibilities. It ranges from the silent screen to Bond...James Bond. One can take a pick of characters, themes, products, ephemera (that paper word again), or bizarre categories like studios, artists, stars, or manufacturers.

Not everything has staying power, however. Watch out for those products that are specifically manufactured before the film releases—a sure sign that they're out to get the quick money (kind of like refusing to allow the critics to view a film before its public debut.) Not every little premium given away at a fast food place is worth keeping.

Notwithstanding the junk and tinsel, the field is great! It has stories, imagination, and weirdness-to say nothing of the people who collect this stuff. We've even seen self proclaimed Jedi Masters with their light swords standing in lines at appraisal shows waiting to convince us they're real.

Guess what? Maybe they are. Maybe we've created an alternative world that is just as vibrant, colorful, and dangerous as the one we live in every day. Maybe that's why people collect the things they do. It gives them comfort, nostalgia, and good vibes. Why, "we might not be in Kansas anymore, right Toto?"

So here's to red slippers and blue suede shoes!

Diamonds Are Marilyn's Best Friend

IN 1953, MARILYN Monroe and Jayne Russell scored with the song, "Diamonds Are A Girl's Best Friend." It was the hit number from *Gentlemen Prefer Blondes.*

But there was another big hit in Marilyn's future. Actually a big hitter. Just around the corner, there was a new romance waiting with one of American's greatest sports heroes.

But before love, disappointment.

Marilyn had hoped that Oscar also preferred blondes. She had her fingers crossed that an Academy Award might be in her future.

No such luck. She wasn't even nominated. Not for *Gentlemen Prefer Blondes*, or anything else…ever.

So instead of Oscar, Marilyn cozied up to a guy named Joe…Joe DiMaggio. He was the king of baseball, and she was the queen of Hollywood.

The crowd went crazy for them.

Nothing but a fabulous wedding ring would have been right for America's "royal couple." DiMaggio gave his bride a platinum eternity ring, encrusted with 35 baguette-cut diamonds.

Diamonds may last forever, but not all marriages follow suit. On October 5, 1954, just 274 days after they were married, Marilyn Monroe and Joe DiMaggio divorced. (That's show biz.)

At an auction of Monroe's personal items in November 1999, the ring sold for $772,500. (That's the auction biz)

Tragic Love Story

JOE WAS MARILYN'S "diamond in the rough." He returned her love with undying devotion. It was rumored that DiMaggio was just about to ask her to remarry him when she passed away.

For twenty years after her death, DiMaggio arranged to have six roses delivered to her crypt three times each week. When he died in March 1999, his last words were reported to be, "I'll finally get to see Marilyn."

Thousands Cheer

After marrying and spending their honeymoon night in a $6.50 motel room, they flew to Japan, where Monroe was to entertain U.S. troops in South Korea. The famous story goes that upon her return to the hotel, Monroe gushed, "Joe, you never heard such cheering!" "Yes…I have," DiMaggio answered.

A Man Is Known by The Company He Keeps

HE WAS A baseball legend and adored by millions of fans. He was given the nickname "Yankee Clipper" by broadcaster Arch McDonald who admired the gracefulness of his play in the field.

And normally, a picture of Joe DiMaggio is a nice collectible. But it's not what you'd call a "big ticket item" at auction.

But add Marilyn Monroe to the mix and we're talking a whole other ball-game.

In the 1950's, after hanging up his uniform, Joltin' Joe's "star status" had begun to fade. But he shot right back to the top. As a matter of fact, he went from "star" to superstar.

It all happened when he hooked up with another bright light from the Hollywood firmament…Marilyn Monroe.

In October 1999, Christie's auction house held what became known as the "Sale of the Century." They auctioned off more than 500 items that belonged to the blonde bombshell.

One was a picture of Joe DiMaggio that had been ripped from a magazine. It sold for $9,500.

That must have given someone's bank account quite a jolt!

Provenance

THE ONE BIG word in the antiques business is provenance. It means the origin or source, particularly WHO owned something. The WHO is very important. The fact that your grandmother owned something may not be very important at all, but if your grandmother was SOMEBODY, then what she owned makes a difference to a lot of people. The item may be identical to what someone else owned. In fact, it may be what millions of people owned, but if that one item was touched by a special someone, then it has a special characteristic. Provenance can transform a simple bag of golf clubs by seismographic proportions. A $500 set of four MacGregor woods and a Wilson 2 wood in a red and white golf bag brought over $700,000. Guess why? Provenance.

The golf clubs belonged to John F. Kennedy. They were sold at the Sotheby's Estate Sale of Jacqueline Kennedy Onassis.

(JFK was good at a lot of things, but he was no Tiger Woods!)

> Those famous golf clubs were purchased by Arnold Schwarzenegger, husband of Kennedy niece Maria Shriver.

Happy Birthday, Hollywood Style

USUALLY A NIGHT at NYC's Madison Square Garden starts off with a song. And that song is our national anthem.

But on May 19, 1962, folks were singing a different tune. They were led by a Hollywood star not generally known for her vocal…shall we say…"attributes."

The "chanteuse" was Marilyn Monroe.

Her throaty, flirty rendition of "Happy Birthday, Mr. President" is one of the sexiest songs ever recorded on tape or film.

The birthday boy? President John F. Kennedy.

Although she may not have been easy on the ears that night, Marilyn was *definitely* easy on the eyes. Accentuating her "positives" was an incredible dress. The fit and fabric had eyes popping from the Garden floor right up to the rafters.

The gown was a full-length, flesh-colored designer original by Jean Louis. It was encrusted in 6,000 rhinestones. The dress was so form-fitting, the actress had to be sewn into it.

> **Oh You Beautiful Doll**
> A collectibles company created a limited edition of 750 vinyl Marilyn dolls. Each collectible figure wears a gown crafted with over 1,300 aurora beads! A button on the base activates a recorded excerpt of Marilyn's sultry birthday song. Don't think many children will be playing with these.
>
> **Leon's Red Flare:** Beware of anything that is marketed as a special limited edition. As Brian and I both say, "If it's originally sold as a collectible, it probably won't be.

(It's amazing she could get enough breath to sing!)

Because of the color and fit, the dress appeared to be see-through. From the right angle, it looked as though Marilyn was "in the buff" and dotted with glittering diamonds.

Hubba hubba!

That dress is still making mouths water, even without Marilyn inside! In 2004, it was sold at auction for $1.2 million! (Those have got to be the most valuable rhinestones in the world!)

It's A Wonderful Life on Sesame Street

Okay, here's a question for all of you movie buffs and Muppet fans out there:

What does the television series Sesame Street have in common with the Oscar-winning movie "It's A Wonderful Life"?

If you answered "frogs and pigs," you're wrong...and have obviously never seen the 1946 holiday classic directed by Frank Capra.

Memorabilia from the holiday classic *It's A Wonderful Life* is very collectible. One collecting specialty is lobby cards. Lobby cards are small, card stock movie posters that were displayed in the movie theater lobby. They showed scenes for the movies they were promoting. Authentic, mint condition lobby cards from *It's a Wonderful Life* are selling for over one thousand dollars.

The correct answer is "Burt and Ernie"...two popular characters that inhabit Sesame Street *and* the town of Bedford Falls.

On "Sesame Street," Burt and Ernie are a lovable pair of longtime friends. One is tall and thin, the other a little shorter and...shall we say...horizontally challenged.

Trivia buffs and old movie fans (like us) know that Muppet master Jim Henson's Bert and Ernie were based on Bert the cop and Ernie the cab driver. Their home: Bedford Falls, the picture-postcard hometown featured in "It's A Wonderful Life."

Rumors that Sesame Street will soon welcome a new pair of long-time friends—Brian and Leon—have been greatly exaggerated.

Double-Dipping at the Oscars

JACK NICHOLSON HAS two... So does Tom Hanks... And Frederic March... And Marlon Brando.

In all, only seven stars have earned "Best Actor" Oscar bookends. Only greats like Spencer Tracey, Dustin Hoffman, and Gary Cooper could boast about a *pair* of Academy Award statuettes.

Seven men with two Oscars each.

But only one man has won two Academy Awards for the same role...and in the same year! That man was Harold Russell.

Russell was a veteran. Not a Hollywood veteran. A *real* veteran. He had lost both hands in a grenade explosion during World War II.

Russell was cast in the 1946 movie "The Best Years of Our Lives" in the challenging and true-to-life role of an amputee struggling with life after combat. He earned a Best Supporting Actor statuette for his heart-wrenching performance.

But the Academy had something more in mind.

Leon's Travel Tip:
Wilmington, North Carolina is the home of Frank Capra, Jr., whose Dad made *It's A Wonderful Life*. The film is shown every year around Christmas at the University of North Carolina Wilmington for free. Frank Jr. hosts the program and offers insight into the personalities of the actors and the making of the movie. Refreshments are offered at the end. Frank Capra, Jr. owns Screen Gems Studios and has either produced or helped with the production of hundreds of movies. Wilmington, nicknamed Wilmywood, and EUE/Screen Gems is the largest full service motion picture facility in the US east of California. Just a word of advice; if you come at Christmas, save us the aisle seat and a bag of popcorn. It's free but they run out!

A Page from Brian's Memory Book
"I had the pleasure of working with Harold Russell and the opportunity to hold those Oscars in my hands. And I'm still holding on to the inspiring autograph that he penned for me. It reads: *It's not what you've lost that counts--Rather, what you have left and how you use it.*"

Russell was honored with a second statuette—a special Oscar. It saluted him for "bringing hope and courage to his fellow veterans."

Is Oscar for Sale???

IT'S TRUE—YOU can buy an Academy Award.

According to the rules of Oscar's "parents"—the Academy of Motion Picture Arts and Sciences (AMPAS)—you're not allowed to buy or sell statuettes awarded after 1950.

Even if you win an Oscar yourself, you have to sign a waiver promising never to sell it, except back to AMPAS. The established "sell-back" price: $1.

But before 1950…it's open season!

So who's buying Oscars? Disgruntled "also-rans"?

Not necessarily.

Stephen Spielberg, a multiple Oscar winner himself, paid $607,000 for the 1934 statuette awarded to Clark Gable for his role in *It Happened One Night* and $578,000 for the 1938 Oscar given to Bette Davis for *Jezebel*.

What's so unbelievable about that? Nothing…except *he gave both statuettes away!*

> **Carbon Dating**
>
> How can you tell the age of an Oscar? Don't cut it in half and try and count the rings!
>
> Just look on the base. In 1949, the Academy started numbering them.

Is Spielberg crazy? Crazy like a fox! He gave the statuettes back to the Motion Picture Academy because he felt that such respected trophies shouldn't end up on the mantle of someone who didn't earn them.

Give that man an Oscar! Oh wait… they already have! Three Oscars AND a Lifetime Achievement Award.

And rumor is that he intends to keep them all.

If I Were King of the Oscars

THE KING OF Pop has won Grammys, MTV Awards, and probably a garage full of trophies, statuettes, and loving cups.

Still, with all the honors he's been given, Michael Jackson has never earned an Academy Award. Although he's never *won* Hollywood's most prestigious honor, there *is* an Oscar at Michael Jackson's house.

(And we don't mean Oscar the Grouch!)

At a Sotheby's auction in 1999, the King of Pop set his sights on the King of Oscars: the trophy awarded to producer David O. Selznick for his masterpiece of American filmmaking…

Gone with the Wind.

In its day, GWTW earned seven Oscars in all. They included honors for Vivien Leigh (Best Actress), Hattie McDaniel (Best Supporting Actress), and Victor Fleming (Best Director). The film also won for Art Direction, Color Cinematography, Editing, Screenplay Writing, and Best Picture

The Selznick Oscar auction turned into a "thriller." Jackson went head-to-head in a protracted duel with a telephone bidder.

But Jackson wanted "the big one." And he was willing to pay a BIG price for it. His winning bid was five times more than the highest pre-sale estimated price.

Sold! For $1.5 million!

A Sotheby's spokesman said the purchase had fulfilled Michael Jackson's "lifelong desire to own that particular object."

Price Aberrations

Appraisers learn to discount extremely high or low prices, particularly when the items are unusual or there is something "fishy" about the results. One auction Leon held years ago resulted in a feud between two buyers. Each obviously hated or disliked the other. When the item they both wanted went up for auction, neither person would back down. The bidding went up, and up, and up. The intensity in the room went up as well. Leon's dad, the auctioneer, understood what was going on, and despite the possibility of earning a very hefty percentage from the sale, stopped the bidding and told the bidders to cool off. He then proceeded to auction other items and came back to the disputed item an hour later. One of the bidders had "wised up" or "cooled off" and it brought what it should have. Not all auctioneers are so thoughtful or conscientious. It could have brought twenty times what it was really worth. When looking at sales results months or even years later, one is usually not privy to all the details. The high figure may be justified, but often it is not.

COMEDY: MAKE 'EM LAUGH

~ ABOUT COMEDIANS ~

"When I told my friends I was going to be a comedian, they laughed at me."
~ Anonymous—or some comedian who forgot
to copyright his joke—I guess?

I DON'T THINK anyone really knows who the first comedian was or when he or she performed the first stand-up act. Perhaps it was some prehistoric man swinging a club imitating the chief of the clan trying to club a wooly mammoth.

But for sure, somewhere during the act along came a sidekick to play straight man to the headliner.

Maybe we haven't advanced that far from prehistoric humor. We can't resist laughing hysterically at home movie clips of someone falling off dock into the water, some dad getting whacked with a piñata stick, and the amazing pratfalls of Jerry Lewis.

Birth of a Nickname

CAN YOU NAME the funny man who went trick or treating in Harlem dressed as Charlie Chaplin? He grew up to become the most beloved figure in early television whether he was in a suit...or a dress.

You've got it! Milton Berle.

Berle was a long-time veteran of vaudeville. And he often dressed in 'drag'...high heels and a Carmen Miranda fruit salad hat.

The wild and crazy guy ruled the airwaves as host of the Texaco Star Theatre. It was NBC's original "must see TV" and ran from 1948 to 1955.

How must-see was this TV?

Well, many theaters and other businesses closed on Tuesday nights. There was no reason to stay open. Most people were home, glued to their 11" screens and addicted to Berle's highly visual slapstick humor. It's believed that Milton Berle was responsible for the sale of more television sets in the United States than any other individual.

This achievement earned him the nickname "Mr. Television."

But it's another affection sobriquet (that's antique-y talk for nickname) that most people associate with the comedian. And it's a name he gave himself.

One night, Berle spoke directly to young viewers. He told them to "Listen to your Uncle Miltie," and go to bed. After that, Mr. Television was everyone's "Uncle Miltie."

Autographed vintage head shots of Uncle Miltie consistently sell at auction for a about $350.00.

From Harlem to Hollywood

HARLEM...KIND OF puts you in a New York state of mind, doesn't it?

Well the Harlem that we're talking about is just as famous as the Big Apple's northern neighborhood, but it's considerably further south...in Georgia.

Harlem, Georgia is the birthplace of one of everyone's favorite funny men: Norvell Hardy.

Not laughing yet? Perhaps that's because you know this turn-of-the-century comedian by another name...one that was usually attached to that of his buddy Stan.

Still clueless? Then here's a hint: The dynamic duo won Oscars in 1932 for the film "The Music Box."

(All of you who think we mean either Batman or Robin because of the "dynamic duo" reference…you're out!)

We're talking about two of the world's favorite "buddies": skinny Stan Laurel and his portly pal, Norvell "Oliver" Hardy! The classic comedians starred in more than 100 films together during their long career.

Stan and Ollie were so beloved that Norvell's birthplace—humble Harlem —became a national shrine. And you'll find their likenesses on collectibles from salt and pepper shakers and to cookie jars.

Laurel and Hardy…we like to think of them as the "Brian and Leon" of their day!

> *Sons of the Desert* (1933), the fourth of Stan and Ollie's full-length feature films, is considered by many (including us) to be their funniest. It's also the name of the duo's international fan club. The organization was founded in NYC in 1964 by comedians including Chuck McCann and Orson Bean. Today there are more than 150 chapters-- known as 'tents'--worldwide.

The Most Famous Comedy Routine in History

NOTHING BEATS A great comedy team. They are a special pair of personalities that create a level of comedic energy that makes you fall off your seat with laughter.

There's always a "straight man" for the 'funny guy' to play off.

The classic team mentioned above was Laurel and Hardy, but the teams that followed, added their own style to the classic comedy team.

Abbott and Costello did great stand-up routines, including the icon of confusion "Who's on First;" the baseball dialog that many have memorized and has been immortalized in the Baseball Hall of Fame in Cooperstown, NY. This hysterical routine has even been licensed as a corporate training video used to teach communication skills.

They made full length movies including the "Abbot and Costello meet…" series. They usually met up with some scary guys like: The Mummy, Frankenstein, The Invisible Man, and other creepy dudes.

Their memorabilia and autographs are collected by many. Here's the collecting tip about comedy teams—The value of Abbott and Costello's autographs on the same photograph can be worth six times more than the value of their separate autographs on individual photos. So don't break up the team. If you are looking for the autographs of the classic comedy team, find one photograph signed by both. You'll end up with the most desirable form of autograph—"the team photo."

The Longest Laugh?

THERE'S A LEGEND in the comedy world that claims that the longest laugh ever recorded is from a routine performed by Jack Benny. It was the "Your Money or Your Life" bit.

Jack Benny, whose on-stage personalty was known as a cheap and frugal skinflint, was 'held up' on stage at gunpoint. The mugger made the demand; "your money or your life." There was a long pause and the robber barked; "I said, your money or your life," to which Benny replied "I'm thinking it over."

Naturally, the place roared, and Benny's routine made the records books—kinda. In reality, it was not the longest recorded laugh in comedy, nor was it the longest recorded laugh of Jack Benny's career. The longest laugh on the Jack Benny show was the result of a blooper made by the live announcer referring the show's sponsor "Jello" as "Jelly." Boy, we just love bloopers.

Jack Benny's persona of a crotchety and cheap man, was far from the truth. He was a kind and generous person who supported many charities. Benny was also an accomplished and talented violinist. He intentionally played poorly on stage to get a good laugh. Thanks Jack!

More Laughs Than a Barrel of Monkees

IN THE MID-1960's, the world was a hairier place…and we're not talking about the geo-political situation!

John, Paul, George, and Ringo had crossed the Atlantic. Their music, as well as their long hair, took American by storm. And in Hollywood, creative minds were desperate to cash-in on Beatlemania.

Producers Bob Rafelson and Bert Schneider sent out the call for four "zany" actor/singers that they hoped could be molded into the next Fab Four. (Think "Spice Girls" with a "Y" chromosome!)

Many were called; few were chosen.

450 wannabes auditioned, but only Mickey Dolenz, Mike Nesmith, Peter Tork, and Davy Jones were chosen to sing, "Hey, hey we're the Monkees."

> Monkees memorabilia is so popular that there is an entire book dedicated to identifying and valuing this pop group's collectibles. Lunch boxes, board games, comic books, gum cards, clothing, buttons, jewelry, sheet music, and even Davy Jones coat hangers, are just items of the thousands of items produced to promote this incredibly popular group.

The Monkees topped the Nielsen and Billboard charts. The series was one of the most-watched programs in television history, and the band had several Top 10 hits.

However they were much less successful on the big screen. Their 1968 movie *Head*—co-written by Jack Nicholson!—is filled with music, psychedelic images, and lots of "insider" references...

But not much humor.

Head was a flop in theatres. But, to this day, it remains a cult hit for die-hard Monkeemaniacs and just generally weird people...

(Not that we know anyone like that!)

MUSIC: THE SWEETEST SOUND I EVER HEARD

~ ABOUT MUSIC ~

"Of all noises, I think music is the least disagreeable."
~ Samuel Johnson

MUSIC, SWEET MUSIC! Musicians—not so sweet. I'll take the music.

Probably the most identifiable music collectible is the record. Ever since Thomas Edison invented the toilet paper shaped cylinder disk, people have been recording and listening to recorded sounds. They've also been buying sheet music and records in huge numbers, spurred on by changes in music styles and cultural tastes.

Admittedly, the most popular and valuable recordings are rock and roll, not the earliest classical ones featuring Enrico Caruso and what's his name…(you see, how soon we forget). The progression from cylinder to 1" thick and flat (one-sided) to 78 and 45 and 33 1/3 was rather slow, giving us time to buy, throw away, and then re-buy our favorites in the same medium. Now that has changed and the CD/iPod era is upon us, providing instant digital access and unlimited choices.

Fortunately, many people like the old vinyl record—and the machines that played them. The covers were artsy. The grooves were "groovy." The sound was…"far out." It's no wonder people will pay big bucks for early Elvis, controversial Dylan, and the "bloody" Beatles. It was OUR time and

OUR music WE got the money.

The times, they are a changing, however. More and more young people have never seen a record, let alone a sleeve. Most have never played a real juke box, and records are becoming white elephants—except in the area of serious collecting.

Records can bring much more revenue than the machines on which they played. Phonographs, even the wind-ups, are nice to own and easy to find, but not high in price—nor are Victorian square grand pianos, Melodistas, roller organs, and the home parlor organ with cardiac pump action. Most instruments fare no better, unless they carry a brand name or master's label.

Even labels are suspect. What better example than the Stradivarius violin? Here's one of the most expensive antiques in the whole world, and yet everyone has one in his or her attic. Guaranteed! Seems that Sears & Roebuck sold them, complete with the hand written label, by the millions around 1900. Today, these copies are worth about the price of admission to a concert at Carnegie Hall.

The end result is that it's not all music to the ears. Be forewarned. This is an area for the learned, the expert, and the extreme hipster. Don't get caught with your CD stuck in an 8-track player. It just won't work. It's a trip you don't want to take!

Not Free to Be Freewheelin'

MOST VINYL RECORDS are technologically obsolete, and you're more likely to find them being used for décor than dancing these days…but there will always be a few albums that are going to be worth big bucks.

Nothing sells like "Censored" and that's exactly what CBS Television did to Robert Allen Zimmerman… Robert Allen who? Perhaps you know him by his "groovier" name…

Bob Dylan.

In 1963, the "voice of a generation" was scheduled to appear on the Ed Sullivan Show and sing his controversial ditty "Talkin' John Birch Blues" but the network said no way, Jose.

(Actually, they said, "No way, Bob.")

"Talkin' John Birch Paranoid Blues" is a fictitious, satirical story about a man joining the society, but it was deemed too hot to handle by the CBS censors. The song was cut. Dylan was so angry that he insisted it also be cut from his poised-for-release album "The Freewheeling Bob Dylan."

Columbia Records complied and halted distribution, but not before a few originals escaped and made their way into the marketplace.

There's no way of knowing exactly how many copies exist. But we do know this: an original "Freewheeling," including the banned song, may be worth as much as $20,000!

That's a lot of green for singing the blues.

> **Brian's Mini-History Lesson**
> The ultra-conservative John Birch Society was founded in 1958 with a stated mission: "Less Government, More Responsibility, and--With God's Help--a Better World." Its un-stated mission was to fight the threat of Communism and other perceived "un-American" influences in the United States...and to promote the free-enterprise system. (Show me the money!)

Jersey Boys

JERSEY BOYS HAVE been making music for generations. Bruce Springsteen... Frank Sinatra...Count Basie...John McCormick...and Enrico Caruso.

But they would never have been heard by millions of fans if it weren't for another Jersey boy—Eldridge Johnson.

Johnson was a resident of Camden, NJ, and in 1901, this music maker founded the Victor Talking Machine Company.

Eldrige cared about how music sounded *and* how music players looked. Around 1905, he began to experiment with a novel idea to disguise the unsightly trumpet that amplified sound in existing phonographs.

When he folded the horn into a large floor standing cabinet, with doors to cover the opening, he made history...and a fortune! His idea was quickly patented and copyrighted as the "Victrola."

Victor would spend $50,000,000 on print advertising and $17,000,000 on catalogs and brochures by 1929. He turned his brand name into a generic name.   Soon the word 'victrola' was applied to all phonograph players designed as furniture.

In 1927, the Victor Talking Machine went to the dogs...or at least to "Nipper," the symbol of the company's new incarnation as "RCA Victor."

Close to 7,000,000 Victrolas were produced between 1906 and 1929. Mint-condition Victrolas are routinely offered on ebay for thousands of dollars. More afford-able 'stored in the attic' machines sell for as little as $200. Oak is usually better than mahogany and table models better than the floor variety. The portable phonograph was actually marketed by Sears & Roebuck as early as the 1920's and looked like a small suitcase. It cost $14.95 and was called the Portola.

A Stradivarius Can Be Yours...For Just $1

FROM 1644-1737 Antonius Stradivarius and his sons made history along with violins. They created the most famous instrument ever made...

The Stradivarius violin.

Only about 1100 of the violins that bore their name were created in their Cremona, Italy workshop. And less than half of those originals remain, per-haps as few as 500.

That makes a true Stradivarius one of the most valuable instruments ever made, too. A true Stradivarius can be worth up to $4 million. (That's music to anyone's ears!)

Have a Stradivarius sitting around in your attic or garage? Think you may be sitting on a goldmine?

Sorry to disappoint you, but...

As people around the world fell in love with Stradivarius in America, another love affair was developing. Companies like Sears & Roebuck and

Montgomery Wards were in love with the idea of cashing in on the Stradivarius craze.

They decided to create machine-made knock-offs.

Before long, millions of copies of the violin—complete with labels and handwritten dates—were being plinked, plucked, and bowed all across the country. You could choose from the $1 model to the "deluxe" $8 version.

So how do you know if you've got the 'real thing'?

Well, you can't judge a book by its cover, or a Stradivarius by its label. First, fake 'authentic' labels were created for the department store knock offs. Plus restorers sometimes stick genuine labels inside instruments of various origins. In fact, labels are a 'business' all their own.

Chances are, your dusty old stringed thing isn't worth much. But the only way to be sure is to take it to one (or more) reputable violinmakers or dealers for an expert opinion.

But there's an upside to all of this: you can still make real music on a fake Stradivarius.

On a First Name Basis

MUSICIANS AND PERFORMERS depend upon their agents and record producers to create a 'brand name' for themselves. Those that manage to be recognized by the world, either with their talent or with good publicity, are in much better position to become rock star icons.

So who are most collectible? They might be 'first name basis' rockers like:

John, Paul, George and Ringo—Beatles

Madonna—well, maybe not lately

Prince—or formally Prince, or used to be Prince—no longer Prince and Prince again.

How about Elvis? What about Christina, Britney, Clay, Rubin, and Cher...or maybe they're music critics like Randy, Simon and Paula.

> Eric Clapton donated many of his guitars to charity auctions to raise money for a drug and alcohol treatment center called 'Crossroads.'
>
> One guitar, Clapton's 'Brownie,' a 1956 Fender Stratocaster used on the *Layla* album, brought over $400.000.00.

All these folks can fall out of favor as quickly as they entered the public eye. So if you are buying or selling music memorabilia, choose wisely. The pop star of today can be falling star of tomorrow.

SCIENCE & TECHNOLOGY: THE HALLS OF SCIENCE

~ ABOUT SCIENCE AND TECHNOLOGY ~

"Science carries us into zones of speculation,
where there is no habitable city for the mind of man."
~ Robert Louis Stevenson

IT MIGHT SEEM strange to have a section on science and technology in an antiques and collectibles book, but without science and technology, most of the items described in this book would not exist.

The technology of the industrial revolution transformed manufacturing processes. No longer did individual craftsman make handmade products, but now items were mass produced in factories and on assembly lines. This change in production is considered by some experts to be the dividing line between antique and non-antique items.

Science and technology play an incredibly important role in the development of manufacturing processes and materials development. Both 'form' and 'function' of some of the world's most valuable antiques and collectibles are the result of applied science and technology of the time.

Evidence of the technological advances made for both consumers and commercial applications can be found in metallurgy, wood finishing, radio technology, automotive advances, air travel, space flight, television and computers.

Some collectors prefer to document technological breakthroughs by creating a collection of 'technological firsts:' first commercial computer, first home video game, first silver plating process, first automobile model, first item flown to the moon.

These timelines of technological discoveries are used by professional appraisers to date, identify, and authenticate (or prove fake) many specialty collectibles and antiques.

There are hundreds of technology collecting fields including computers—the first Apple computer is highly prized. Automobiliana traces the roots of ground transportation. Cameras and photography capture the progress of visual arts, projection systems and movies. Radio collectors fall into many categories: radios with tubes, radio with transistors, and radio with integrated circuits.

So, study the progress and development of technology and science, and you will become a more savvy and confident collector.

Don't overlook science fiction, because today's science fiction may become tomorrow's science fact.

Jolly Old Sheffield

DID YOU KNOW that there's a "silver" out there that isn't really silver, but is as good as gold to some collectors?

It's Sheffield silver…or more precisely Sheffield plate—a "technological revolution" in its day.

Old Sheffield Plate was invented in a small town in jolly Old England as a substitute for sterling. You can find it in shapes and styles that were almost identical to the sterling pieces of the same period.

Sheffield "silver" isn't rotten to the core…but it isn't silver to the core, either.

The Sheffield plate process takes very thin sheets of silver and hand-solders them over a core of copper. It's the age and rarity and beauty of Sheffield pieces that make them valuable collectibles despite this "core issue."

Old Sheffield Plate was served up in 1750 and popular for sixty to seventy years until a shocking discovery was made.

Electroplating!

When American silver "smartie" William Rogers discovered electroplating, an electrical process that could lay on microscopically-thin layers of silver cheaper and faster, Sheffield lost his sheen.

Electroplate was faster and cheaper…but not better.

Similar to sterling silver, Sheffield plate is known for its pleasing, warm color. There is a pride of craftsmanship in the creation of Sheffield. It requires artistry, patience, and the human touch.

In short, Sheffield is a philosophy while electroplate is just a process.

So remember: Sheffield may not be sterling silver, but it's definitely a 'golden' collectible. And valuable, too!

It's Magic

LONG BEFORE GREEN screens and computer-generated images, there was a different kind of movie 'magic'…the magic lantern.

The magic lantern was the 'Internet' of its day…the most advanced piece of technology in existence. It took people on a magic carpet ride to see and learn things far removed from their daily lives.

Kits of slides and narration booklets on a variety of topics: history, geography, science, religion, and natural science, were sent to schoolteachers, ministers, and town officials to share with their followers.

So how does it work? Like magic…old-fashioned magic. Magic lanterns use technology that has been around since the days of the Pharaohs.

Egyptians created a 'magic' box with a light that would project through a semi-transparent image onto a screen. Think of it as the great-granddaddy of the slide projector or overhead projector.

The very first magic lanterns were lit by candles, then by kerosene lamps, and ultimately by Mr. Edison's electric light bulbs. Electricity was cleaner… and considerably safer…so that yelling 'Fire' in a crowded theatre was a less common occurrence!

Peck and Snyder, a company with great influence in industry, sold at least forty seven different varieties of magic lantern. On a popular antiques TV show, one machine, in excellent condition, was valued at between $1,000 and $1,500.

Most magic lanterns have values in the hundreds, rather than the thousands of dollars. But, it's the small glass slides themselves that are the big money items. The hottest and most valuable are those depicting scenes from the Civil War. Some have been sold for more than $3,000 each.

Now that's what we call 'magic.'

Are You Listening?

UNLIKE US, YOU may think of days before the Internet as "the Dark Ages…" If that's the case, you'll probably consider these next collectibles from our childhood to be relics from prehistoric times.

(Or perhaps that's what you think we are!)

But don't kid yourself, once upon a time, when Little Orphan Annie was really little and when technology was a shiny new penny to spend, the hottest thing on the block was…

The radio.

The radio was meant as entertainment for the masses. So they were mass-produced and priced very affordably. And they're still affordable today.

You can get prime collectibles from Admiral, Coronado, Silvertone, and Westinghouse for a song! The price for radio brands sold at popular chain stores is still just somewhere between $10 and $40.

BUT…tune in to this!

High-end radio is on a whole other frequency. Table versions in glass or with Lucite cases were made by companies like Addison, Atwater, Kent, and Clearfield. They were extremely expensive and that made them exclusive.

That exclusivity, along with time, has made these "voice boxes" extremely rare. And collectors have made them extremely valuable. Some sell for more than $2,000!

Leon says, "According to my notes, the 1934 Zenith Stratosphere…a 23-tube console model…may be worth more than $3,000!"

Anyone want to try for four?

The Grandfather of Radio

SURE, EVERYONE KNOWS that Guglielmo Marconi is the "father of radio," but did you know that there's a *grandfather* of floor model radios?

Yup. There sure is.

Introducing the late, great Sparton 1186 "Nocturne," a sleek combination of glass, metal, and wood from 1936.

Times were tough during the Depression. (No kidding!) So designers, marketers, and manufacturers formed an alliance to make "fashion" part of the appeal of industrial products...from radios to refrigerators.

Ads described the ultra-modern Nocturne as "A circle of midnight blue Tufflex mirror glass rests in a satin chrome cradle...Beautiful state setting for High Fidelity receiver cleverly concealed behind the chrome barred grille."

Standing nearly two feet high and wide, the Nocturne was designed to be the focal point of its setting. It was meant for a hotel lobby or other commercial building.

When it was released in 1936, the Nocturne was priced to sell—to the rich and successful only. At $375.00, it wasn't for an "average Joe."

Not then...and not now. The Nocturne is the single most coveted and most expensive of all Art Deco radios. Less than ten are known to exist...each with a value of more than $7,500.

> Radio models can tell us the age of almost any radio. Our research files contain all kinds of information on old radios. We track the model numbers of many different old and antique radios. Each manufacturer published a catalog which listed a description and the model number of their radios. When someone asks us for the value of a radio, we can identify the year by getting the model number and referring to our catalog research file.
>
> So, do old radios play those old radio shows?

Did They Mean 7-11?

A RARE GLIMPSE of an excerpt from Brian's bizarre research notes:

When I came across a set of silver flatware marked 18/8, I thought I'd really stumbled onto something. I figured it was a rare, valuable, collectible *misprint* from the House of Slurpees, also known as my neighborhood 7-11.

No such luck.

It was actually a reference to that old silver impersonator, stainless steel. Stainless looks like silver, but it's not. It's really an alloy.

What's an alloy? It's a mixture. And the alloy known as stainless steel is a mixture of chromium, nickel, and steel.

(This info tidbit comes to you courtesy of the New Jersey Institute of Technology. That's where I became a chemical engineer.)

The 18/8 mark that I uncovered was a description of the composition of the steel. IT represents the percentage of chromium and nickel in the allow.

Who developed this pretender to the throne of authentic silver? An Englishman named Harry Brearley (another chemical engineer, by the way!)

Brearley was experimenting with new alloys that could better resist the erosion caused by high temperatures in WWI military weaponry.

But that was just the beginning.

Brearley had cut his eyeteeth in the little old town of Sheffield, famous for the manufacture of cutlery. So it was only natural that when little Harry grew up that had an appetite for turning his new invention into mass-produced knives, forks, spoons, and more.

Ya gotta love it.

It's clean, sleek, and contemporary—and with no need for a polishing cloth or elbow grease. Stainless steel may not be silver...or even silver-plate...but it's on our 'solid gold' list.

~ Notes From the Appraiser's Notebook ~

How To Identify A Qualified Appraisal

APPRAISALS SATISFY A variety of needs and legal requirements. At some point in our lives (or at perhaps at the end of them) we will all need the services of an appraiser. How well this appraiser provides his or her service will directly impact your financial status, tax liability, insurance needs, buying decisions, and perhaps how much time you spend with an IRS auditor.

This article will cover the very basics of appraising, appraisals and appraiser qualifications for personal property.

You're in the Top 2%!

AFTER YOU READ this article, you will know more about the requirements of a qualified appraisal than 98% of those calling themselves appraisers. That is a very frightening fact.

In addition, there are no laws in place in any state, as of the writing of this article, for personal property appraisals. Anyone can call himself or herself an appraiser—another frightening fact.

The responsibility of selecting a qualified appraiser falls upon you.

An appraisal is formal, written documentation of the research and reporting of a specific value for a specific intended use. It must be an unbiased, qualified, arms-length report. Appraisals must not be misleading and must report a value conclusion based on proper research and accepted appraisal methodology. Dealers and collectors may be very familiar with the prices of manuscripts, rare books and autographs, but few know the appropriate and required procedures for presenting these values in an appraisal report.

The report must be written so that the client and any third parties will understand the process and procedures used in arriving at the value conclusion stated. All readers of the report must understand any limiting conditions and critical assumptions that may be a part of the assignment.

Qualified appraisers must act with impartiality, objectivity, and independence. Likewise, they must carry out their duties without accommodation of personal interest. They must avoid any action that could be considered misleading. That means they must avoid any possible "perception of impropriety."

If this is true, (and it is) then why are so many dealers offering to provide "appraisals" of the material they sell to their customers?

Based on these standards, an "in-house" appraisal does not meet the criteria of a qualified appraisal. If it is written for the "intended use" of determining insurance coverage, for example, it will most likely be rejected by a knowledgeable underwriter because it might not be unbiased or impartial.

Even if it is accurate, the *perception* of impropriety still exists.

The IRS guidelines are even more strict. (You know the government!)

Recently, an autograph dealer acting as an appraiser provided an "appraisal" of a portion of an estate consisting of many presidential autographs. After the appraisal was completed, the dealer purchased the autographs at the appraised value. The IRS heard of the transaction and negated the entire estate appraisal including real estate, fine art, and the residential contents. The trust officer had to hire a new appraisal team, pay interest and penalties, and resubmit the estate paperwork.

Guess who was sued for the cost of penalties, interest, and the cost of additional appraisers? Yup...it was the dealer/appraiser who was on the wrong end of that suit.

In addition, the appraisal did not cover the minimum requirements of the appraisal profession let alone the IRS standards. The IRS will next look to see if the appraiser attempted to undervalue the collection. If so, the estate is responsible for a minimum penalty of 30% of the underpayment, plus the tax and the interest.

Don't Let This Happen To You

IF FRAUD IS proven, the appraiser, the trust officer, and the estate are subject to additional penalties.

The following list will provide you with an idea of what questions to ask potential appraisers.

- What formal tested training has the appraiser taken?

- Can he or she provide the documentation to back it up?

- Twenty years in the autograph business is no indication of appraisal competence. Nor is a degree in history. Historians, archivists, and curators are not necessarily appraisers. Look for appraisal qualifications.

- To what professional appraisal organizations does the appraiser belong?

- Are they tested members or can they become a member by just writing a check? You can call the organization to find out if they are active and what classes they have passed.

- The three primary organizations are: The American Society of Appraisers, The American Association of Appraisers and the International Society of Appraisers.

- Can they provide a sample report for your review?

They can and should have a sample available. Check it against the Appraisal check list below.

- What is their area of expertise?

Appraisers cannot be experts in all fields. Recently, an appraiser told me she did "baby bottles to battleships." Oh yeah? How many battleships do you think she appraised this year? An appraiser must know his or her limitations.

- Do they consult others?

If so, who do they use as associates and what are their qualifications?

How do they research the market?

Many "appraisers" guess, or look at auction results and dealer catalogs. That is certainly not enough. The appraiser must know if the item actually sold and who bought it. Did it sell to a dealer or a retail collector? How many people were at the auction? Was it bought back? What is the scope of their research? In our office, we maintain over 1,476,000 records of manuscripts, rare books, and collectibles. Each item is cross-referenced by subject, date, condition, and content.

- Do they subscribe to an appraisal standard? Do they know what that standard is?

All of these requirements should, if followed, result in a qualified appraisal.

To meet these standards, our appraisal reports, for example, contain thirteen pages of information in the cover letter alone. The cover letter and the body of the report describe the markets selected, the methodology utilized, the appraiser's qualifications, the appraisal dates, the value being reported, the limiting conditions, the compensation method, and any critical assumptions that may be a part of the assignment.

As you may notice, the primary focus of the appraisal is on describing what value conclusion is being provided, how that value was researched, what methodology was employed, and why the appraiser is qualified to report that value. Anyone can report a value. Only a qualified appraiser can back that value up with research, defensible expertise, and formal training.

Selecting an appraiser can be a long and tedious process. Reviewing an appraisal also takes great time and effort. The alternative however, is to take your chances and pay the potential consequences later.

Pay now…save later. It's the only way to fly with appraisals.

~ Appraisal Checklist ~

A written appraisal, by anyone, should include:

- The "use" or "function" of the appraisal—e.g. to obtain insurance coverage, to establish tax liability, etc.

- A detailed description of the specific property being valued

- An analysis of the factors that affect the value

- The date(s) of the valuation, the inspection, and the report

- A statement of the appraiser's qualifications

- A statement of financial disinterest (no conflict of interest) and fee policy (no surprises)

- Any limiting conditions or critical assumptions related to the value conclusions

- The appraiser's certification and signature

Battling Appraisals

RECENTLY, LEON AND I both had assignments to appraise drop-leaf tables.

The two pieces were very comparable. But Leon's was appraised much higher than mine. And both values, though different, were accurate.

How could that be?

My work was being done for an insurance appraisal. Leon's was being done as part of a bankruptcy proceeding. Insurance replacement cost is researched and reported based on the retail market. Bankruptcy value is based upon a forced sale. So there are different values for the same item.

But wait…there's more!

When it comes to estate tax liability… that's based on fair market value. And running business equipment… that's value in place.

That's a lot of different values that can be assigned to the same piece! So appraisers refer to the value *reported* as the "purpose" of the appraisal. The *reason* is called its "use" or "function."

To get the best, most accurate appraisal, follow a policy of "Do ask" and "Do tell." Instead of just asking, "What's it worth?" Be sure to tell your appraiser the reason you're asking. By the way, a professional, qualified appraiser will ask you how you intend to use the report, and produce the appropriate report for your needs.

You'll get a response based on your "need to know."

~ Brian

Color Me Valuable

RECENTLY I ASKED Brian if he'd ever heard of "patina." He wanted to know if I was talking about an Italian opera singer.

When I asked him to think "Oldies But Goodies," he started singing an old Frankie Avalon tune.

I explained 'patina' didn't have anything to do with Frankie Avalon, Frankie Sinatra or Frankie Valley... But that thinking about the "Four Seasons" coming back year after year was an excellent hint.

Turns out he was pulling my leg. (Oh Brian, you trickster!)

Brian knows what patina is...and now you can, too...

Patina refers to the color and texture of a surface that occurs with age and years of handling. Edges grow smooth...hard outlines are softened... (Sounds like what happened to me when I turned 50!)

A great patina increases the value of any item.

Israel Sack, the famous New York antiques dealer, defined it best for one of his senior female patrons when he said:

"Today you are a lovely woman of 60. However, who you are today is not who you were when you were 20. The difference is patina."

~ Leon

My Lesson In Diamonds

BEFORE I KNEW better, I figured the price of the diamond reflected its quality. I thought "The Four C's" that diamond appraisers use when grading diamonds were "Cost, cost, cost, and cost."

Leon set me straight.

He told me that every appraiser uses "The Four C's" to grade four different characteristics of a diamond. He said that the C's refer to Cut, Carat, Color and Clarity.

Unfortunately, that left me with a fifth C…as in clueless.

Leon continued my lesson: Cut is the shape of the diamond…like round, pear, or oval. Carat refers to the size of the stone. Clarity expresses how perfect or "brilliant" the diamond is.

The fourth C had me stumped…color. At that time, I thought all diamonds were clear or "white."

Who knew (Leon did!) that natural diamonds come in an absolute rainbow of colors? And some of them are extremely valuable…especially when they travel in groups!

Maria Menounos, the Entertainment Tonight host of the 2004 "Oscar Arrivals" telecast, wore a gown encrusted with a waterfall of 2,000 breathtaking champagne-colored diamond stones valued at $2.5 million.

Well, color me surprised!

~ Brian

Can You Spot A Fake? (We Can)

FORGERIES AND FAKES abound in the antiques and collectibles biz.

An itty-bitty mark can mean the difference between a few dollars for a fabulous fake and thousands of dollars for the genuine original.

Brian and I both know that art glass names such as Galle, Steuben, Lalique, and Tiffany are particularly suspect because they're easy to fake with a paper label, engraving tool or rubber stamp.

You need protection! You need an appraiser.

There are a couple of things we do to make sure that what you see is what you think you're getting…and not a fake.

First, we research how the original marks are supposed to look. A lot of would-be forgers take marks from catalogues and advertisements that were never actually used on the items.

Original marks are usually sharp and clear, despite their age. Surprisingly, the new fakes look fuzzy or unreadable.

Another dead giveaway is a misspelling or an incorrect placement of a mark…the kind of thing an appraiser would spot, but that an "Average Joe" (or Jane) might overlook.

Sometimes the best way to save money is to spend money. With an appraiser, you'll know what you're getting before you buy it. And that can mean the difference between investing in the real thing and throwing your money out the window on a fake.

~ Leon

Getting Personal

PERSONAL PROPERTY APPRAISERS are a strange breed…

Some are part-time dealers, some are auctioneers, and some are simply private collectors of antiques and memorabilia. A lot of them are nice folks, but they're not necessarily qualified to give you an accurate value for an item.

A few are "bad seeds"… The only thing they know is the best way to take advantage of ignorance. And, unfortunately, many are very good at that.

Now Leon and I are a strange breed, it's true. But we're also *qualified* appraisers. We know antiques and collectibles, *and* their value.

We've been trained, tested, and certified in the methodology, principles, and techniques of appraising various items. And, like all the best things in the world of antiques and collectibles, we've stood the test of time…

We're "tried and true." And that's important, because there is no such thing as a "licensed personal property appraiser," and there are no state laws to regulate those who are in the appraisal business.

When you're having your valuables appraised, you don't want someone who's "learning while earning." You want an accomplished pro on your team.

One way to separate the white hats from the black hats is to check an appraiser's credentials and membership in professionals associations. Just remember these letters. They spell "the best":

AAA — Appraisers Association of America

ASA — American Society of Appraisers

ISA — International Society of Appraisers.

NAJA — National Association of Jewelry Appraisers

Okay! You're on your way to finding a "Brian and Leon" near you!

~ Brian

You Don't Need To Be From Kentucky

IN MY AUCTIONEERING day, I could have been known as "Colonel Castner," even though I'd never served in the military.

How come?

Turns out some of the first auctioneers were colonels… Civil War colonels dividing up the spoils of war.

You see, after a battle, the conquering army needed a way to parcel out everything of value. Auctioning personal property (and everything else) to the highest bidder seemed to be the answer.

Traditionally, the person responsible for army property was the colonel of a unit, and he was "pressed into service" as the auctioneer.

Colonel is just one of the names that auctioneers have been identified with over time. Other names include "Knights of the Hammer," and "Brothers." And even though they weren't called colonels, they still wore a colonel style hat.

Today, some schools that license professionals in this field award the title of "Colonel Auctioneer." They may not get the hat but they do get the rank.

Well shut my mouth! (Not likely!)

~ Leon

~ About the Authors ~

Leon Castner

"Appraising is no longer a guessing game by people who think they know prices. It is a science of valuation dealing with appropriate methodology, principles, and practice."
~ Leon Castner

LEON'S AN AUCTIONEER, appraiser, writer, speaker, and even was featured on ABC's 20/20. He holds a Ph.D. in Valuation Science and is a Senior Partner of National Appraisal Consultants, a firm specializing in personal property appraisals and appraisal consulting, insurance reports & research, pretrial consultation, and IRS tax-related appraisal matters.

Leon is a Registered Contractor for RTC, FDIC, the US Marshall's Office, the Attorney General, and TASA. He has provided major appraisals for these organizations. He is also the co-presenter of Appraising the Appraisal—a professional development seminar for insurance agents, claims managers, and trust officers, and is a Panel Member of the American Arbitration Association. He holds a CAPP in Appreciable Residential Contents and has served as an adjunct professor of Fine and Decorative Arts at Centenary College.

Leon is also past Chairman of ISA Designation and Review, and past President of the New Jersey Chapter of the International Society of Appraisers. He has been honored by his peers with The Auctioneer of the Year Award by the New Jersey State Society of Auctioneers and has received the ISA's Outstanding Member of the Year Award.

With Brian, he co-hosts a weekly radio program *Value This!* on Oldies 1510, and webcast live on www.WRNJ.com

Brian G. Kathenes

"The more we can learn about the things and events of the past, the greater our opportunity to create a wonderful, exciting, responsible future."
~ Brian Kathenes

BRIAN HAS BEEN the keynote speaker at the Folger Shakespeare Library and at the Library of Congress in Washington, DC. He is the past chairman of the New York Winter Antique Show Vetting committee with Leslie and Lee Keno (of Antiques Road Show fame).

Brian was also the on-air TV appraiser and science fiction / technology consultant for the Discovery Channel's collectibles show: POP NATION: America's Coolest Stuff.

He has appraised the Batmobile, the Back to the Future Car, and memorabilia from the blockbuster movie *Titanic*, including the giant ship model. Brian has appraised items that have been on the Moon, and even appraised (and played) Elvis' guitar.

He's an Eagle Scout, so you know he'll always tell you the truth, and was honored as *Hope Township's Outstanding Citizen of the Year*.

Brian is the past Chairman of Ethics for the International Society of Appraisers and was the First Director of Education for the Universal Autographs Collectors. He is a member of the American Philatelic Society Appraisal Committee and served as an expert witness in the Nixon Watergate Papers Trial.

With Leon, he co-hosts a weekly radio program, **Value This!**, on WRNJ Oldies 1510, and webcast live on www.wrnj.com

Value This! with Brian and Leon

Value This! is a weekly call-in talk show that covers everything you wanted to know about antiques, collectibles, and memorabilia…and a few things you didn't! Hosted by Castner and Kathenes, who say they have "perfect faces for radio," the show is filled with wit and wisdom and lively segments such as "What's It Worth" and "Stump the Appraiser."

Loyal and enthusiastic listeners, many of them hooked on Brian and Leon as much as the information that they share, have catapulted *Value This!* to the top of the ratings where it has remains a leader. The show has enjoyed three years as the #1 radio program in its AM market (WRNJ Oldies 1510) and is now heard live on the web at www.wrnj.com

~ Bonus Section ~

Our Gift To You!
Free Bonuses and
Special Offers from Us to You!

~ Bonus #1 ~

Get Free Monthly E-News Tips On The Inside Secrets

Get free monthly e-news tips on the inside secrets to finding bargains galore at flea markets, antique shops, and garage sales. You'll receive collecting tips from the sharpest appraisers and dealers in the country. And it's free! Signup at www.BestAntiqueTips.com.

Or complete this page and mail it to:

Brian and Leon's Bonus #1

National Appraisal Consultants

P.O. Box 482

Hope NJ 07844

Or Fax it to: (908) 459-4899 (fax this page)

Name: _____

Address: _____

City: _____ State: _____ Zip: _____

Phone: _____ e-mail: _____

~ Bonus #2 ~
Learn How To Become A Professional Appraiser

Visit www.AppraiserSuccess.com
and sign up for your free appraiser e-news

You will receive special "appraisers only" e-mails on tips
for building a successful appraisal business

AND You'll get our special report:
"10 Easy Ways to Boost Your Appraisal Sales
& Increase Your Client Base in Less Than 30 Days"

It's a $49.00 Value and it's your free!!

Or complete this page and mail it to:
Brian and Leon's Bonus #2
National Appraisal Consultants
P.O. Box 482
Hope NJ 07844

Or Fax it to: (908) 459-4899 (fax this page)

Name: _____

Address: _____

City: _____ State: _____ Zip: _____

Phone: _____ e-mail: _____

~ Bonus #3 ~

Be Famous!! Get Your 15 Minutes Of Fame
On The Radio!!

WE WANT YOU to be a "Radio Star" on *Value This! With Brian and Leon*, our weekly radio program. We're live and on-the-air every week on Oldies 1510, WRNJ AM and on www.wrnj.com.

Here's what you do:

- Visit our Value This!! Radio Website at www.ValueThisRadio.com

- Listen to the show on WRNJ—Oldies 1510 AM or on the web at www.wrnj.com. If you can't listen live don't worry, there's a button so you can download a show to listen to.

- Decide what item of yours you wish to ask about.

- Call **(877) 4-1-VALUE** and leave a message for our producer. Our producer will call you back and tell you when we'll be calling to put you on the air.

- Sit back, relax, and share your item with us and our listeners. We'll answer your questions on the air and you'll be our special guest.

- Brag to your friends and family about how you're a big radio star.

OR

E-mail me your questions to TheUglyGuys@BrianAndLeon.com

~ Bonus #4 ~

Be in the Next Edition of
Betcha Didn't Know That!

Here's an opportunity to be a part of the next edition of *Betcha Didn't Know That!*

There are two ways to be a part of the next "Betcha" book.

One: Read through this edition and let us know where you find typos and errors. Some are intentional and others are not, but if you find them and send them to us, we'll give you an editorial credit in the next edition.

- Or -

Two: Send us your collectibles stories, tips and factoids. If they meet our editor's review, we'll add them to Volume 2, and we'll give you credit for your contribution.

Send your submissions and discovered typos to:

Betcha Didn't Know That!
P.O. Box 482
Hope, NJ 07844

Betcha Didn't Know That!

Gunnar H. Kathenes

Livingston resident was Navy veteran of WWII,
president of vehicle supply company, 88

Gunnar H. Kathenes, 88, passed away at his residence on Saturday, Oct. 12, 2013.

Family and friends are invited to the Restland Memorial Park Chapel, 77 DeForest Ave., East Hanover, N.J., on Friday, Oct. 18, at 10:30 a.m., followed by the funeral service at 11 a.m. The committal service will follow.

Born in Bergen, Norway, Gunnar arrived in the United States in 1930, settling in Bloomfield, N.J.

He and his beloved late wife, Peggy, moved to Livingston, N.J., in 1952.

He was employed by Richard G. Pfeiffer, Inc., Orange, N.J., and retired as its president in 1989. After retiring, he continued working for the Franklin Miller Co., Livingston.

He was also a former assistant scout master for Troop 19, Livingston.

During World War II, Gunnar was a Navy torpedoman's mate third class. By virtue of his service, he received the Presidential Unit Citation as well as the American Theater Medal, Philippine Liberation Medal, and the Asiatic-Pacific Medal with five stars.

Surviving are his devoted children, Brian and wife, Nancy, Jaime, Holle, Sean; and his loving grandchildren, Colleen, Tyler and Lee.

In lieu of flowers, memorial contributions may be made to ProjectUSE, 23 Pennsylvania Ave., Newark, NJ 07114, www. ProjectUSE.org, or the Livingston First Aid Squad, 62 S. Livingston Ave., Livingston, N.J. 07039.